PRAISE FOR 40 YEARS IN THE WILDERNESS

"A compelling read! With remarkable courage, Yiscah tells the story of her struggle to reconcile the depth of her connection to her Jewish tradition with her yearning to express her true female self. This groundbreaking book offers an authentic view of how, after forty years of wandering through her life as a traditional male, she finally comes home as a woman."

~ Hadiyah Carlyle, *Torch in the Dark: One Woman's Journey*

"This is a beautiful spiritual memoir of an amazing woman. Yiscah's story gives me new ways to understand the meaning of courage, trust, reliance on G-d, and what it means to live an authentic Jewish life. I could not put the book down and I learned new insights at every turn of the page. I recommend this book to anyone on a journey to authenticity and to G-d."

~Rabbi Gail Diamond, Associate Director and Director of Institutional Advancement, Conservative Yeshiva of United Synagogue, Jerusalem

"40 Years in the Wilderness is a passionate account of self-realization in terms of both gender identity and Judaism. In Yiscah Smith's journey, living as a woman and living as Jew are equally necessary, intertwined paths through the wilderness that lead into profound relationship with her Creator."

~Joy Ladin, *Through the Door of Life: A Jewish Journey Between Genders*

"I was simply riveted reading the pages of Yiscah Smith's powerful and heart-wrenching memoir. Her story is of three difficult personal journeys, which mixed and complemented and clashed with one another. The journeys were from entrapment in a man's body to a full, rich life as a woman; from a secular life and disoriented Jewish observance to a meaningful spiritual life within the Jewish tradition; and from a life of wandering to a true home in Jerusalem."

~Joel S. Migdal, *Shifting Sands: The United States in the Middle East*
Director Interdisciplinary Ph.D.
Program in Near & Middle East Studies,
Robert F. Philip Professor of International Studies,
Henry M. Jackson School of International Studies,
University of Washington

"Yiscah Smith's immediate, authentic voice shines through every step of the story of her life. It is a story of tikkun olam. We will always needs stories of people who endure and rediscover their place in life, and celebrate it to the fullest; the world needs these stories, and Yiscah Smith has given us one to cherish.

~Dr. Richard A. Sprott, co-chair of the Children, Youth and Families Committee of the Society for the Psychological Study of Lesbian, Gay, Bisexual and Transgender Issues.

Forty Years in the Wilderness:

MY JOURNEY TO AUTHENTIC LIVING

Yiscah Smith

Wooded Isle Press

Printed in the United States of America

Library of Congress Cataloging-in-Publication Data
First Printing, 2014
ISBN 978-0-9916623-0-2

Wooded Isle Press
2400 NW 80th Street, #272
Seattle, WA 98117
woodedislepress.com
CIP/LC pending

Cover Designer – Naama Ozair: Dahlia Graphics
Author Photograph – Dovid David: D2Photography

DEDICATION

Mom, this book is dedicated to you (may you live and be well), and to your mom, Grandma "Brooklyn," of blessed memory. You both taught me by example what it means to unconditionally love and nurture. The both of you were always unquestionably there for me and always supported me, even when I was not there for myself. The both of you always made me feel special, even when I didn't feel that way about myself. The both of you made me feel my dreams could and would come true—and they are!

And the both of you as well inspired me to know what it means to be a woman. Each of you modeled for me the ideal combination of grace, dignity, gentleness, feminine beauty, and poise mixed with inner strength of character and integrity. You both loved being the women God created you to be, and you inspired me to feel the same—and now I do.

The Baal Shem Tov taught that each of our lives comprises forty-two journeys, corresponding to the forty-two journeys the Children of Israel experienced in their forty years in the wilderness. Some of these journeys have pleasant names. Others don't sound so nice. But none are inherently bad. It is only that you may have to dig deeper and deeper to find the purpose and the good within them.

CONTENTS

PREFACE

The story I tell is one of a man, facing his truth, embracing the woman she was always meant to be, and returning to her faith with wholeness and authenticity. I believe my story must be told. It is important for everyone to hear and will hopefully inspire and empower many others who face seemingly insurmountable obstacles to wholeness in their lives.

My story is not simply a tale of personal triumph over inner demons. Rather, I am telling my story in order to, with the help of God, inspire and help others who are mired in obstacles—people for whom achieving a life of authenticity, genuineness, and wholeness feels impossible. I, like many individuals, was paralyzed by fear, shame, and low self-esteem for most of my life. Like me, these individuals find themselves unable to make the leap of faith they need to honor their own inner truth. Many people, deep inside, yearn to somehow catapult past their personal demons, the forces strangling, suffocating, and wringing the life out of them. My demons were gender identity disorder and the passionate desire to live a spiritual life within the Jewish tradition that conflicted with it.

Specifically, my book targets Jewish people, gender variant or not, who struggle with issues of being authentic within the Jewish community. For these individuals, finding a place for themselves within themselves and among other Jews is painfully difficult. They feel discriminated against, disconnected, and marginalized. They sense their soul urging them on to live a spiritual life in the Jewish tradition, but feel excluded by the very Jewish communities they wish to join. Rather than being welcomed and included, these Jewish people feel pushed away and rejected.

Any human being who struggles daily to be honest with him- or herself can benefit from reading my story. Imagine what it would be like for that person to wake up one morning and live the entire day as a personal testimony to his or her inner truth.

How many people can honestly say they do not compromise their own inner integrity in order to be accepted, to be respected, to be included, to be counted as a member in the club, and to be loved? How many people fail miserably in their attempt to experience self-worth by living other people's expectations of themselves, seldom expressing their own essential being and core? How many individuals yearn for camaraderie with friends who will love and respect them for who they truly are and not for who they appear to be? And how many individuals seek role models, teachers, mentors, and peers who can inspire them to in fact experience this space of honest and authentic living?

My book may, just may, help one of these individuals. It is for that one individual I am writing this book—the Jew, the gender variant, or any human being who wonders how he or she can go on one more day living a life that belongs to someone else, a life that is tragically not their own.

As the Jewish tradition teaches us, "Whosoever saves a single soul, Scripture ascribes merit to that person as if the person saved a complete world" (Talmud, Sanhedrin 37a).

PROLOGUE

WHAT IS, ISN'T, AND WHAT ISN'T, IS

I could not have been older than five years old. However, it's as if this occurred minutes ago, forever etching an indelible impression on my psyche, my heart, and my soul.

My parents were preparing to go out for the evening. My beautiful and graceful mother, projecting an energy of warmth mixed with the epitome of feminine elegance, was picking out her jewelry for the evening and applying her makeup. I happened to be in their bedroom at the time. The most natural response for me was to do what I did—I stood there, gazing in awe as my mother began to adorn herself, as her inner grace and glow were revealed through her physical beauty. I was entranced by this ritual and hoped that this moment would never end. I felt so happy, so right, so normal, watching my mother prepare herself to go out for the evening, intent on learning everything I could so when I grew up I could and would do the same. No daughter could want or expect a better role model.

Suddenly my trance came to an abrupt halt. While not malicious, it was vicious and startling, waking me out of my perfect little five-year-old world where everyone lives happily ever after. Without warning, my mother candidly and yet firmly directed me in the guise of a question: "Why don't you go into the bathroom and watch your father shave?" The door to the master bathroom was open, and my father had just stepped out of the shower. His towel wrapped around his waist, he was shaving his face, performing his own manly ritual of grooming.

Not only did it never occur to me to watch my dad rather than my mom, but when my beautiful and well-meaning mother suggested, rather strongly, that I watch my father instead of her, the only response I could offer was "Why?" What part of me would rather watch my father shave than gaze at my mother putting on her makeup and choosing her outfit, jewelry, and shoes?

Her answer pierced my heart, and then, as if it were a sharp knife increasing the pain, it turned and turned within my heart and ruthlessly woke me out of my imaginary world. Simply and clearly, with utmost authority, she said, "Because you are a boy."

Why would she ever say such an untruth to me?

How could the woman who conceived me in loving intimacy with my father, who carried me for nine months and felt me grow within her womb, who gave birth to me, who nurtured me with unconditional love and devotion to my well-being, who would sacrifice her life in an instant to spare me harm, and who glowed with pride every time she looked at me, be so utterly and completely wrong? And how could I, a five-year-old child who worshipped the ground she walked on, who watched every move she made when I had the chance, who felt so protected by her protectiveness, tell her so?

Her answer made as much sense to me as it would have if she had told one of my two sisters the same. However, there was a major difference between my two sisters and me. When my mom would bathe each of my two sisters and dress them, she saw them as little girls. My parents would talk to them, play with them, shop with them, and behave toward them the way most parents at that time did with their toddler daughters. And when my sisters looked into the mirror, the mirror reflected back what they expected to see. They were girls.

For me, however, everything was different. Everything seemed to be turned inside out, topsy-turvy, upside down. Different in such a cruel and confusing way. I likewise expected to see the mirror reflect back to me what my sisters did, but it did not! Instead it reflected back to me the body of a little boy. My parents spoke to me as if I were a boy. My family at large, the same. My community, my teachers and classmates, and the world kept messaging to me a fundamental mistruth about myself. The mirror lied, my parents lied, my birth certificate lied, everyone and everything lied to me about my gender. And they had no idea of this perversion of the truth, nor how much this not only hurt me but led me on a path of serious ill health. After all, how can one five-year-old doubt the entire world, never mind challenge it?

How is it possible that a little five-year-old girl could be so right about herself in spite of all the evidence to the contrary? And yet I intuitively knew, with the same clarity and surety, that I must keep my truth a secret. Living in such secrecy only magnified my sense of estrangement from myself, and from everyone else. I began to live in fear—afraid of becoming close with anyone, and equally afraid of not becoming close with anyone.

At this point in my childhood, I became acutely and painfully aware that something was not right with me. Something inside me warned me to be quiet, to keep this terrible, uneasy sense of myself a secret, a secret from everyone around me. I even tried to keep this a secret from myself, but always in vain. This awareness haunted and seriously challenged any hope I had for a typical happy, secure childhood. I was disconnected not only from the world, but from myself. I did not know what to do with this chronic gnawing truth, other than keep it to myself. How I wanted these feelings about myself to leave me alone so I could be like every other child—normal!

* * *

If a man stands facing the Western Wall in the Old City of Jerusalem to the extreme right, as far as he is allowed, and a woman stands likewise facing the Western Wall to the extreme left, as far as she is allowed, they will find themselves only inches apart, separated by the mechitza, the physical divider between the men and women.

In June 1971 I found myself at the Western Wall in the Old City of Jerusalem. I was a twenty-year-old man, painfully approaching from the left.

Forty years later, in June 2011, I again found myself at the Western Wall in the Old City of Jerusalem, a woman, proudly entering from the right.

My story is the journey of a soul—my soul. My forty years in the wilderness. My forty years of moving only a few inches from the men's side of the mechitza on the left to the women's side on the right. I spent forty years traversing countless peaks and valleys, parched deserts and lush oases, journeying and living, leaving Jerusalem, returning to Jerusalem, living in Jerusalem, leaving Jerusalem again, and finally returning home to Jerusalem. More than anything in the world, I wanted to return home, without even knowing what home would be. It took me forty years to move a mere few inches.

Jewish mystics teach about the individual's experiences of both exile and redemption. While exile and redemption play pivotal roles throughout Jewish history, the mystics taught that these were personal spiritual, emotional, and mental states of being as well.

The phrase "What is, isn't, and what isn't, is" defines the painful experience of my own personal exile—exile from the real "me," whoever that was, exile from living an authentic life—enslaved and paralyzed by the taskmasters of fear, self-doubt, and despair. For most of my life, I projected a self-delusion, a lie. I lived in this chronic state of exile for the first twenty years of my life, and on and off, to one degree or another, for the next thirty years after that.

Only then, at the age of fifty, did I begin to experience inner redemption. In the space of my gender transition, I began tasting relief for the first time in my life. I recognized my inner truth, and then embraced it, honored it, and lived it. Contrary to running away and living in a false illusion, this personal redemption helped me begin living in a profound state of simplicity and spiritual health. So new to me, so foreign to me—and yet, it felt so right, so light, so clean. The open wounds of deception, manipulation, lying, shame, and fear began to heal and transition into well-being. After a forty-year journey, I was finally becoming myself.

PART ONE

CLARITY AND CONFUSION
1971–1979

Chapter 1

THE FIRST STEP

My forty-year journey into a personal wilderness began on a June evening in 1971. I boarded a charter flight to Frankfurt, Germany. Daring, different, and new, I traveled alone, with no itinerary. My plans did not sit well with my parents, who seemed overwhelmed with concern. Any attempt at convincing them that there was nothing to worry about was predictably met with resistance. They anxiously pleaded with me to rethink this "crazy irresponsible idea."

However, this was anything but a mere whimsical, fleeting idea. A tugging from within urged me to do this. I felt I was running, moving, entering uncharted territory. Was I being pushed or was I being pulled? Was I was running away from myself in utter despair or was I running toward myself in utter despair? Usually, I went along with the majority, terrified to strike out on my own. I had the option of hitchhiking cross-country to San Francisco with some friends of mine for summer vacation, but I elected not to join them. The push and pull of making my own way was too strong to be ignored.

The decision to travel by myself to a new part of the world, without a specified itinerary, defied my very own life experience and stood in stark contrast to anything I had ever done before. I actually startled myself, and had I thought about this plan for too long I may very well have canceled the entire trip. Perhaps for the first time in my young but torturous life, I decided to do what I intuitively sensed I needed to do. This inner tug was so strong I was unable to resist its incessant urging.

After I purchased the ticket, I actually felt relief. Relief transformed into excitement as I imagined journeying into a foreign and unknown future. I became a daydreamer. For the first time in my life, I felt excitement rather than dread about what lay ahead tomorrow. Once I had the ticket in hand, I don't recall a moment when I thought to cancel the trip or to ask others to join me. I felt determined to do this, and to do this alone.

Many years would pass before I could thoroughly enjoy my own company, but in deciding to travel alone I began to feel the joy of pure excitement and unbridled anticipation. Again, I surprised, even alarmed myself! I possessed no context within which to relate to these new feelings. Intuitively, I sensed that something other than my own will urged me to travel and journey ahead. While not apparent at the time, I allowed this "other" force to simply remain a mystery for the time being.

Imagining how to make the most of a few dollars a day in Europe filled me with a sense of wonder and adventure I'd never experienced before. The southern European and Mediterranean countries intrigued me and captured my attention. My imagination took over as I thought about all the cities, villages, and beaches that lay ahead for me to explore.

And yet, I intuitively sensed once again the voice from deep within calling out to me. Another country beckoned me to visit and experience her. Clearly it was not Germany. The only clarity I had about landing in Frankfurt was that I would leave for my first destination outside Germany as soon as possible, for, although I was not raised in a traditionally observant Jewish home, my family and the Jewish community we belonged to expressed utter contempt for that country. I resolved to remain open to the possibilities of a new destination, never expecting it to become apparent within a few hours of takeoff.

My parents said good-bye to me at the airport with loving hugs and kisses and, with tears in our eyes, I assured them I would be fine. Somehow I truly believed that I would. I promised them I would send postcards and letters each week so they would know where I was and that I was well. Now en route to unknown destinations, among other backpacking, adventure-seeking students, I was left to my own devices. What would I do when I landed in Frankfurt? Other than my adamant resolve to leave Germany as soon as possible, I never gave this much real thought. After all, wasn't that what it meant to travel without an itinerary?

Not too long after soaring high into the skies above the Atlantic, I took out a packet containing a wealth of travel information I had collected. I eagerly began to peruse the many brochures, imagining what my days would be like. I would be exploring the museums and galleries in Paris and the countryside in southern France, camping in the Swiss Alps, sunbathing and swimming at the beaches in Spain, visiting more museums in Italy and its beaches as well, touring the remains of ancient Greece. This would be followed by visiting some of the many Greek islands about which I heard so much. "Wow," I said to myself, "this is amazing. I can actually go to any of these destinations, or all of them." My heart would be my tour guide and lead the way. My mind would follow.

Or, as a whisper within me suggested, none of these countries! Did I hear myself correctly?

I arose from my seat as if beckoned by this same gentle but clear whisper. I then proceeded to do something that would profoundly change the rest of my life. This one act would greatly affect my family members, some of whom were yet to be born. As well, what I was about to do would impact countless other people with whom I would connect over the years. Indeed, it was a crucial moment in my life, in my family's, and in many others' lives. The profundity of this moment, in both its sheer spontaneity and clarity, could never have been just a mere suggestion or contrived thought. With no hesitation, I took this big packet of dreams, walked to the back of the plane, and threw it all into the garbage.

Instantly I realized I had no need for this abundance of information. Without really knowing in my mind, my heart was seeking an experience. Information was not what I thirsted for. Experience, yes!

I knew exactly where I would go after deplaning in Frankfurt. I became vividly and suddenly aware of that unknown destination that had eluded me before. I would book the next available flight to Israel on El Al Airlines. Israel!

It was almost unbelievable, but it was clear. Why would I go to Israel? I was not a Zionist. I was not religious. I hardly knew anything about Israel, nor did I know anyone who had ever traveled there.

That year in college I had learned about the kibbutz, a collectively owned agricultural settlement. The kibbutz way of life idealized communal Marxist living in its purest form, and to my liberal, progressive, idealistic twenty-year-old mind, it was alluring and incredibly compelling! The kibbutz represented the perfect place where I could immerse myself in a social group without ever being discovered for who I really was. It was a perfect escape from myself in an environment that diminishes self-identity and instead emphasizes the collective identity. Custom tailored for me. And where would I find a kibbutz to do this? In Israel, of course! I needed to volunteer and experience life on a kibbutz. With relief, I imagined that this would be so engaging that I would not have time to think about what usually consumed my thoughts—estrangement from myself and from everyone else around me.

Within days I realized both how right and how wrong I had been. I was mistaken not about going to Israel, but for the reason I was going. Israel, absolutely yes. Working on a kibbutz, absolutely no.

Chapter 2

SOME WALK ON THE TARMAC, OTHERS KISS IT

To my disappointment, it would be a few days before the next available El Al flight to Israel. I vividly recall how much it pained me to hear the many people around me speaking German. This was the language with which those despicable butchers, who murdered six million of my Jewish brothers and sisters and six million additional precious human beings, communicated with one another. I could not wait to leave. Every second in Germany at that time seemed unbearable to me.

While still in the airport I met a small group of fellow travelers who were en route to Israel as well. In fact, we would be on the very same flight. What a "coincidence"! They suggested I join them for the next few days, and I gladly accepted their invitation. No one could ever have predicted that my decision to say yes would affect the whole trajectory of my life. The wheels of providence were busily turning, and I had not a clue. We spent the next few days in Frankfurt together, and tried to enjoy the time, although we were all impatient to leave and fly to Israel.

Right away I sensed a special connection with one of the women. This was odd, actually discomfiting. As a woman who felt trapped in the wrong body, I quite naturally felt attracted to men. Socially, I was more at ease and comfortable with other women. But I sought romance and intimacy with men. While the world would tell me I was gay, I knew this not to be true. Of course, I was not gay! After all, I was a woman. Therefore, this connection that I felt with Susan just added more confusion to what was by now only too familiar. What harm could a little more confusion be? Never in my life would I have dreamt or imagined the magnitude of the answer to this supposedly rhetorical question.

Again, "coincidentally," Susan mentioned that she had cousins living on a kibbutz and I would be welcome to visit them with her. This was almost too good to be true. Less than twenty-four hours earlier I had had no idea what country I was headed toward. Suddenly, I decided to go to Israel, met a wonderful person, and accepted her invitation to visit her family on a kibbutz just north of Tel Aviv. All in the "blink of an eye." Why would I turn such an offer down? Maybe this was meant to be. I had never given much credence to the idea of providence, but now I was open to the idea. Meant to be or not, it sure seemed like a great idea.

A few days later, our plane touched down at Ben Gurion Airport. In an instant I was flooded with unexpected and raw, diverse feelings. Anticipation, excitement, fear, joy, sadness, celebration, and gratitude—yes, gratitude, a feeling new and unfamiliar to me. Since when does an almost twenty-year-old from an upper-middle-class family in Long Island, New York, feel a sense of gratitude? And yet, I did. As the El Al plane touched the ground, a round of applause broke out, enveloping everyone on the plane in a state of ecstatic joy that was palpable and emotionally moving. This needed no interpretation. Never before had I witnessed such an outburst of unrestrained applause upon landing an aircraft. It was a life-altering moment. In just a few seconds, I began to realize that Israel holds a unique place in the world. What an understatement from such a place of naïveté!

As the plane taxied on the runway toward the arrivals terminal, I noticed the many billboard signs in Hebrew! This was a language I was forced to learn in the years leading up to my bar mitzvah. I could read it, yes, but without ever understanding it. Still, when I found myself recognizing letters and words and being able to read them aloud, I felt proud and accomplished. Hearing Israelis on the plane speaking Hebrew actually excited me. I was astounded by this proof that Hebrew was a modern language, and not just the stuff of suburban bar mitzvahs. It was already exhilarating to be in Israel, and we hadn't even left the airplane yet!

As we descended the steps onto the tarmac in the blasting humid Tel Aviv summer heat, I witnessed a sight unimaginable. Several men and women, who seemed otherwise like "normal" adults, were actually getting down on the ground and kissing the tarmac. They kissed the tarmac with undeniable expressions of joy and gratitude, uttering what I imagined to be some form of prayers. Tears of joy mingled with oil, grease, and dirt. What a sight to behold! The word pilgrimage came to mind, but Jewish people don't do that…or so I thought. I was in a state of utter disbelief.

Nothing in my life had prepared me for this sacred moment in time. I then understood that I was not walking on just any tarmac in just any country. Although I had not an inkling as to what made Israel special, I knew I had to find out. The inner voice deep within assured me I would.

Chapter 3

THEN WHY AM I HERE?

My first few days in Israel were spent visiting Susan's family. I was immediately struck by their genuine warmth and hospitality. The ease with which they extended themselves to me made me feel genuinely comfortable. Usually when I was a guest in someone else's home, I experienced an unsettling feeling of formality, an awkwardness, and a sense of forced behavior. I seldom felt at home in others' homes. How could I? I did not feel at home within myself. But here, it was as if I had come home, not to a foreign country or to a home filled with complete strangers. It was a surprise I gladly welcomed.

They did very little to accommodate me. You might even say that I received no special treatment as their guest. And yet, I felt a true sense of ease, warmth, and belonging in their home. Unlike anything I had ever experienced, I felt special, loved, and safe here.

Only later would I come to realize that this genuine and warm openness typified much of Israeli culture. Refreshing and new to me, I realized that this was how I aimed to live my life. Although my inner turmoil gave me no respite, my core values included the betterment of humanity and the commitment to advance the quality of life for others. While I had little hope that my own inner well-being could ever be advanced, I idealistically believed that at least I might help others achieve this. It seemed to me, in the short time I'd been in the country, that Israeli culture held those same values. Eventually I would come to understand that these were fundamentally Jewish values as well. For now, I reasoned that if someday I could play even the tiniest role in this culture, then maybe I would be spared from further personal distress and despair.

For anyone who loves the sea as I do and feels more comfortable with saltwater in her lungs and sand between her toes than not, this collectively owned settlement was paradise. Susan and I were welcomed in the spirit of a true homecoming to Kibbutz Sdot Yam, which means "the fields of the sea." For a moment I actually felt that these people were my own family and the kibbutz was my home. I experienced kibbutz hospitality in a number of memorable ways: eating meals together in the communal dining room, visiting the children's houses, drinking midday Turkish coffee with an elderly Sephardic woman, watching with others as the late afternoon sun dipped slowly below the Mediterranean horizon and greeted the dusk, and chatting in broken Hebrew/broken English with various kibbutz members and volunteers.

Halfway across the Atlantic, I realized that I wanted to volunteer on a kibbutz without ever having given it serious thought before. After visiting this kibbutz for just a couple of days, I now knew that this had to be the reason I so suddenly decided to visit Israel. I felt compelled to volunteer on a kibbutz, and Sdot Yam was the ideal one.

My heart skipped beats anticipating the thought of working on Kibbutz Sdot Yam. So exciting, so thrilling. Experiencing communal life in its simplest form, and as a bonus, living by the beach, sounded too good to be true. I was so upset and disappointed when the volunteer office told me that the kibbutz was turning potential volunteers away. The summer of 1971 saw more young people pouring into Israel to volunteer on kibbutzim than ever before. Supply greatly exceeded demand. There simply was no room.

The next day, disappointed but determined, I made my way to the National Kibbutz Volunteer Office in Tel Aviv. Maybe, just maybe, one spot existed for me—on any kibbutz. I received even more disappointing news. Not one single vacant spot on any kibbutz in Israel was available. On the verge of tears, my desperate pleas to volunteer my body and my time went unheeded. At that point I would have gladly accepted any position on any kibbutz, as I felt both dejected and desperate. I was shattered! After all, this was the reason I came to Israel! Where else would I feel so strongly about cleaning toilets and weeding gardens under the hot summer sun (for free!) while sleeping in a one-room corrugated aluminum "house"? A suite at the Ritz Carlton would not compare to what I sought.

Even worse, now I had to figure out what I would do next.

Strangely enough, as I walked out of the office, I began to feel that this dream of working on a kibbutz, all encompassing as it had been just moments ago, was simply "not meant to be." Until this time in my life, I had never thought in these terms. Was I gaining an optimism that allowed me to turn rejection into opportunity? Or was it the voice of denial coaxing me into invalidating how utterly devastated I felt? After all, up until now, denying my own perception of reality was only too familiar. Or perhaps it wasn't "me" speaking to me at all. But then who or what was suggesting this?

Regardless, if I was not meant to work on a kibbutz, then why was I in Israel?

Chapter 4

THERE'S NO PLACE LIKE HOME

Dejected, I traveled to Jerusalem. Visiting the "city of gold," coveted by world empires for several millennia, eased the disappointment I experienced when leaving Tel Aviv. I resigned myself to not working on a kibbutz—this time. Ready for more adventure, Susan decided to explore the unknown future with me. This was another decision that affected both of our lives, and many other lives, for years and even generations to come.

With Susan by my side, I had a chance of masquerading (to the world and to myself) as a man who was falling in love with a very special woman. At such an early stage in my life journey, I had no idea a woman could feel platonic love toward another, similar to two sisters. My own desperation to be included in the world and freed from the mire of low self-esteem and ongoing self-doubt led e astray to disguise my increasing love for Susan as that of a male lover. The unspoken, clearly horrific pressure to meet my family's expectations, my community's expectations, and the world's expectations of me exacerbated my inability to be honest. Most tragically of all, I had deceived even myself. I believed I was experiencing real, romantic love. But deep down, in those rare moments of facing my authentic self, I knew I was lying to myself, Susan, and everyone else around me. Then I would panic, and quickly close the door to this deeper part of me out of fear and shame.

In such a short time, I had experienced so much. I had ventured forth into the hustle and bustle of Tel Aviv, spent time with a family living in one of its suburbs, and visited a kibbutz on the Mediterranean coast. But I was still wholly unprepared for what I was about to encounter in Jerusalem, Israel's eternal city.

Nothing in my education—religious, historical, or political—had given me a context within which to experience Jerusalem. I could not connect to Jerusalem from either the biblical vantage point or the modern Zionist one. The history of Israel is a history I knew nothing about. Furthermore, I never learned of the modern Zionist history of the State of Israel. My experience of Zionism was limited to our community's annual Jewish National Fund drive to collect funds from American Jews to plant trees in Israel. I approached the city of Jerusalem with an utter lack of basic knowledge about her.

The bus began its climb up the Judean hills. Susan pointed out the old reddish rusty tanks on the side of the road. Today they serve as memorials for those young Zionist soldiers who perished at the hands of the Jordanian army during the War of Independence in 1948. Before departing the newly declared State of Israel, the British made sure to equip the Jordanians with a cache of artillery that misled them both into believing they would annihilate the fledgling Jewish state in a matter of days. They believed that the end of the British Mandate meant the genocide of the Jewish population in its own homeland.

We stepped off the bus, and immediately the diversity of the city mesmerized and captured me. So many smells, styles of dress, languages, music, and foods. What an incredible onslaught of stimuli. So much to see, to hear, to feel—and this was all in the central bus station! Tel Aviv was something of a Hebrew Manhattan, so I did not feel like so much of a foreigner there. Jerusalem seemed completely otherworldly—suspended in its rich history while simultaneously teeming with vibrancy.

Immediately I sensed this initial barrage of diverse sensations as a paradox. Dwelling in the space of paradox was all too familiar for me. However, in this particular paradox, I experienced neither pain nor confusion. Rather, it filled me with relief and hope! Externally, Jerusalem was radically different from any other city I had ever visited. Yet, internally, I felt connected and at home with Jerusalem's rhythms and energies, with its spirit and soul. Two opposing sensations competed for my attention, with the internal one easily claiming victory.

Jerusalem itself welcomed me and, as if Dorothy's yellow brick road was laid out in front of me, I moved naturally and enthusiastically through its streets. I imagine I fell in love with Jerusalem from the very first moment I inhaled its air. Something so evident, strong but not overwhelming, welcomed me into its unique environs. It was as if I was seeing life through a different lens—a lens of depth and clarity, and also spirituality. A lens that had escaped me until this sacred moment in time. I could not see it with my eyes, but I felt it, and only later did I come to appreciate that this is what the Jewish tradition refers to as kedusha—sacredness and holiness.

Amazing—an entire city enveloped in kedusha, and I had access to it through this unique lens. I heard Dorothy echoing, "There's no place like home. There's no place like home." For the past twenty years, I had never felt at home anywhere. Now I was overjoyed with a sense of Jerusalem opening up her arms and hugging me. I felt I had returned home—home to a place I've never been. I asked myself if I could really be entertaining such thoughts! And surprisingly enough, without any hesitation, I replied, "Yes!"

Not too long after arriving in Jerusalem, I knew I had to make my way to the Old City, a walled area composed of what appear to be endless narrow winding alleyways, with various gates allowing entry and exit. The Old City stood in stark contrast with the modern city of Jerusalem. As I entered the Old City through one of its ancient gates, I felt as though I were in a time machine, speeding through more than twenty centuries of history. One image quickly replaced the one before it: two glorious Temples, the Greeks attempting to Hellenize the Jewish population, Roman persecution and expulsion, the Byzantine presence, the rise of the Moslems, the Ottoman invasion, the British Mandate, the War of Independence in 1948, Jordan occupying the Old City, forcing the Jews out of their homes and razing the Jewish Quarter to the ground, the Six-Day War in 1967, and Israeli forces liberating the Old City and the Temple Mount from the Jordanian occupation. Then came the arduous task of rebuilding the Jewish Quarter, integrating modern city planning to ensure adequate water supply, sewerage, gas, and electric utilities while simultaneously preserving the ancient flavor and architecture of the original houses, synagogues, shops, and narrow winding pedestrian alleys. It was visually and intellectually overstimulating and invigorating to walk through the Old City for the first time.

Until that first day in Jerusalem, I had no idea about the modern-day miracles that led up to the Israeli army liberating the Jordanian-occupied section of Jerusalem in 1967. Jewish people were once again allowed to visit and pray at the Western Wall, the only remnant of the Second Temple, destroyed by the Roman Empire in the year 70 CE. This may only be a wall to some, but to the Jewish people it serves as both a reminder of the glory the Jewish people once experienced more than 2,000 years ago and a source of encouragement and hope for future global redemption. Jewish people identify the Wall with the belief in universal peace. A belief that remains steadfast and constant. How could I not know this? Was I so absorbed in my own misery that this escaped me during my high school years? To my disbelief, I did not recall ever having learned any of this.

I acquired these basic facts on the spot, with Susan. In the Old City I became aware how modernity had robbed me of experiencing a link to my own personal past. Growing up on Long Island in the 1950s and '60s, an "antique" was something that dated as far back as the turn of the 20th century. Here, the gates' most recent exterior walls are close to 500 years old. Walking through one of the Old City gates and maneuvering through the meandering and crowded pedestrian streets in the open-air market enveloped me in a world that both startled and intrigued me. I was innocently attacked by an immense variety of new smells, sights, and noises. Scores of shopkeepers selling meats, fruits and vegetables, spices, candy, clothes, jewelry, and all kinds of souvenirs were coaxing potential customers in Arabic, Hebrew, English, and assorted other languages. I felt compelled to walk, listen, view, behold, stop, gaze, and simply allow myself the experience of being enthralled with each moment.

I then entered the Jewish Quarter, which was then undergoing extensive restoration. Rebuilding the old proved to be an incredible challenge for the city planners. I could not but help equate that this in fact was what I needed—extensive personal restoration and rebuilding of self. The Jewish Quarter captured me as it became my mirror. The Jewish Quarter as a macrocosm reflected back to me the microcosm of myself, vigorously seeking its own renaissance and rebirth. Could I ever go about rebuilding myself, rebirthing myself with such vigor?

The government's efforts to infuse the Jewish Quarter with new life while maintaining the flavor of an era dating back centuries had me spellbound. I too was beginning to feel an infusion of new life within me, likewise with the flavor of an ancient tradition. In a sense, my own soul had been razed by enemy forces, occupied by a foreign oppressive power, and was now undergoing its own extensive restoration project.

In my life, I have gone on many types of walks. I've walked from one room to another to retrieve something. I've walked along the beach, in forests, and along mountain trails, immersing myself in the wonders of nature. I have walked at a brisk pace, wanting to leave a place or arrive at a place as fast as I could. At times I've walked in a daydream stupor, not even really caring where I am going and when I will arrive at my destination. Yes, my two legs have carried me in many different ways as I have moved from one place to another.

However, walking through the Jewish Quarter to the Western Wall was unlike any walk I had ever taken before. Step by step, with intention and with focus, I experienced moments so inspiring and memorable that they have stayed with me forever. Each step bubbled over with new sensations and fresh sights. This walk afforded me long-sought relief from my acute sense of fragmentation. This walk afforded me the novel experience of being transported back to a time far away from the self that languished in a state of confusing disconnection and spiritual atrophy. It was as if ghosts of the past led me along the way. This pervasive and powerful energy encompassed me in an incredible space never experienced before. For the first time in my life, I became immersed in a space that was greater than the sum total of my own inner agony. I ceased to feel myself. I was enthralled and excited to be experiencing the ultimate getaway—a getaway from myself. A getaway moment that breathed new life into me. All that was clear was that I wanted more of these exquisite moments in time—many more. Was it possible?

I imagined what it would be like to someday live in a community whose sacred traditions dated back centuries and whose history dated back thousands of years. Little did I know that in fact this was destined to happen several years later. Little did I know then how true it is that there's no place like home.

Chapter 5

NOT JUST "A WALL," BUT "THE WALL"

As I descended the first level of steps from the Jewish Quarter in the Old City of Jerusalem to the Kotel, the Western Wall, I froze. I was not able to budge, nor did I want to. This was a moment in time that could not be contained within a sixty-second minute. This was a moment of such splendor and magnificence that it tugged on me to never let it go and to never forget it. My eyes beheld a view that echoed another time that has profoundly influenced, and even defined, world history. The walk through the Jewish Quarter may have transported me back centuries, but what my eyes now gazed upon transported me back almost 3,000 years! All I could do was stare, behold, and savor the moment—a moment in time that repeats itself each time I have retraced these steps over the past forty-two years.

Staring me in the face was the Mount of Olives. This ancient cemetery, which was named for the olive groves that at one time covered its slopes, has been used as a Jewish cemetery for close to 3,000 years. From biblical times through today, Jewish people have been laid to rest here. Here I was, a completely confused young woman held captive in her male body, a baby-boomer child from Long Island, staring at a cemetery where over 150,000 Jewish people have been buried dating as far back as King David. Its sheer grandiosity, both physically and historically, captured me.

Beyond this, I felt as if 150,000 of my Jewish ancestors were welcoming me to the most sacred place on earth, beckoning me to return home. Return home? My home was in New York in the United States, and yet, the sense of being hugged and gently coaxed to return to a different type of home was more than a false illusion or suggestive thinking. It was both genuine and soothing, two emotions I seldom experienced.

After finally breaking my gaze at the Mount of Olives, I then looked north, to the left, and could not believe my eyes. How utterly startling! This was a ride in a time machine that Hollywood producers could not imagine in their most creative moments. Why? Because this was not a fictional screenplay adapted from a novel. Rather, this scenario began almost 3,000 years ago and repeats itself endlessly to each pair of eyes that freezes its gaze upon it, as I did at that moment. I now beheld the most sacred site to the Jewish people—the Temple Mount, upon which the two Holy Temples stood.

This experience both astounded and perplexed me. I seemed to know nothing of the people whose legacy I had inherited. I also felt that as I was being transported back to these ancient biblical times, I no longer suffered my own gender disconnect. In those ancient times, it was clear I was a woman and the idea of being held captive in a foreign male body simply did not exist—at least in my mind.

And then I saw it! Below the Temple Mount was a wall. No! Not "a wall" but "THE Wall!" This very same Wall, while only a remnant from a time long past, has inspired the Jewish people for centuries with hope, encouragement, and a vision. A vision into the future characterized by national as well as personal spiritual enlightenment and eternal global and individual healing.

If I could live within this powerful testimony to both Jewish history and the Jewish future, maybe, just maybe, my own inner problems would magically and miraculously disappear. So, now the moment had arrived. It was time to descend the lower level of steps leading to the Western Wall plaza and touch these sacred stones for myself.

Approaching the Western Wall thrust me into the very consciousness that frightened me the most in my life and caused my chronic daily anxiety. The walk to touch the stones for myself, a powerful source of gratitude and thanksgiving for hundreds of thousands of Jews over the past 2,000 years, plunged me into the confusing mire of a definitive and absolute binary gender system. Here there was simply male or female, with no room for anything in between. Visiting the Wall requires separation of men and women—so simple for most, but heart wrenching and dreadful for those of us who, at birth, entered the world where this was anything but clear. There was no flexibility, no blurring of the clearly drawn lines. I felt forced to choose, to announce to the world whether I was male or female. Males to the left, females to the right.

If I'd chosen the women's side, where I knew I belonged, I would have aroused unimaginable, extreme attention. If I were to choose the gender that the world defined for me, and that to which my body tragically acquiesced, I would have likewise aroused all sorts of unimaginable attention, albeit internal. By now I had trained myself to pervert my own sense of truth into a disguise, allowing the world's mistruth about me to direct me as my guide. And so, to the left I went—excited to touch the stones and despising myself once again for not being authentic and genuine, especially at Judaism's most sacred place.

Equally well trained in denial mechanisms, I embraced each step to the Wall as an opportunity to relish a moment of time where my gender confusion may have not even existed. Ah, the power of imagination!

As I drew closer and closer to the Wall, each of the stones grew in both physical size and significance. They dwarfed me and yet drew me closer and closer. I experienced the sensation of being in a magnetic field, utterly helpless to resist its pull. I looked to my left and right to see how others behaved when directly in front of the Wall. How is one expected to behave? What do I do when my face is so close to the stones that every time I inhale and exhale I can feel and even hear my own breath? What is expected? One touches the Wall. One kisses the Wall. One not only touches the Wall, but affectionately, with care and intent, caresses it. One not only kisses the Wall, but glues one's face to the Wall after kissing it. A touch, an embrace, a kiss that one dreaded breaking. I wanted, I yearned, I sought with hunger and thirst to experience such closeness and intimacy. But with whom? Of course, with God! With HaShem—literally meaning "the Name."

Closeness and intimacy with God was never something I had considered. I had not a clue what this meant, entailed, or implied. To complicate matters, I knew enough to realize that one can approach intimacy only by being authentic and genuine. Nothing about me at that moment, aside from my yearning to live in truth, was authentic and genuine. What the men around me saw was a lie, my lie. How could I dare think I was worthy of such a deep connection?

Yet, here I was. Not knowing what else to do, I imitated those around me, and for the first time in my life, I gently touched and caressed the Wall in this sacred space and time, and then I kissed it. I kissed what appeared to be a stone. A huge stone, a pretty stone, one that bore and continues to bear witness to history, but nevertheless, a stone. I felt the stone gently touching my hands, my face, and my lips in return, as I experienced a warmth that was both foreign and yet familiar. Such a completely new experience, as if HaShem actually greeted me personally and uttered the words just echoed by 150,000 of my people buried in the Mount of Olives: "Welcome home." I sensed I belonged here. I sensed I was dwelling in a space of encouragement and protection. I felt loved, and I felt embraced by the source of love. This sacred space messaged to me that while I lived in a fragmented and strife-torn inner world, restoration of a unity experienced somewhere in my past was now possible! Oh, how I wanted to believe this! Oh, how I was desperate to believe this invigorating and redemptive idea. And a part of me in fact did. Immediately!

I touched and then kissed my past, my present, my future, my people, and my soul—all at once. And my past, my present, my future, my people, and my soul all at once embraced and kissed me in return. On a conscious level, this was my first real intimate moment with my own spiritual center, my soul. In that sacred moment, I knew that for the first time I had encountered pristine truth, in its most vulnerable and naked state, void of all rationalizations, veils of denial, and garments of fear and shame. Did I know what this implied? Did I even know what this meant? Of course not. But intuitively I was aware that I possessed the secret to this hidden knowledge. All I could pray for at that moment was that I would never forget this moment of spiritual awakening and infusion of vigor, of hope, and of encouragement. What else could I pray for? I could have prayed to be praying from a place of truth. I could have prayed to embrace the truth by somehow being the impossible—being that which had evaded me for the past twenty years, being authentic and genuine. But this was far too frightening. I was not yet ready to truly come home. For now I was excited to begin the journey, having no idea where it would lead.

I had approached the Wall so torn up, my integrity so painfully compromised. As I slowly backed away from it, I was still tormented, but now I felt inspired, energized to discover and learn about another part of me that until now had been ignored in its state of spiritual latency. My spirituality was bursting to be acknowledged, to be embraced, and to find expression.

But just as quickly as I found myself focused on a part of myself beyond gender, I sadly remembered a fundamental truth. Judaism is a culture strictly for males and females. I knew right there, at the most profound place to the Jewish people, that somehow I must be given admission into this world and not be excluded. I was determined not to spend the rest of my life as an outsider looking in from a distance. I could not be relegated to an observer status, forced to merely watch my own people's destiny unfold. They are my people. I am in direct lineage to those who have been pouring out their hearts and prayers without compromise in this very spot for the past 2,000-plus years. And yet, how? How could a woman trapped in the body of a man enter? Through which gate?

I left feeling dejected, rejected, and barred from admission. However, a voice from deep within urged me not to fall into despair. This voice urged me to seek, to explore, to inquire—and to beseech with intent for help from the very being with whom I needed to achieve a lifetime relationship of connection and intimacy.

So yes, I began at that moment to dwell in the paradox of both rejection and encouragement, in the irony of living within personal fragmentation and yet sensing that unity could be restored to this miserable state of exile. I left the Wall feeling a sense of pride and gratitude for being born Jewish that both startled and energized me. I now felt purpose and commitment, beyond the mundane struggle to survive. I may not have been ready yet to honor the true feelings of my heart, but at the very least, for the first time in my life, I made a commitment to learn, to celebrate, to inquire about, and to experience my Judaism. If for now it would be relegated to the cerebral experience, so be it. That was in and of itself a huge undertaking for me, and it was the most I could do at that time.

Chapter 6

MY FIRST REBBE, AND HE SINGS, TOO!

The word rebbe, which means "my master, teacher, or mentor," is derived from two Hebrew words, rav (rabbi) and sheli (mine). It connotes one's spiritual leader and guide.

In one of Judaism's classics, The Ethics of the Fathers, we learn, "Make for yourself a rav" (chapter 1, Mishnah 6). The ancient sages realized early on in the development of Jewish values and ethics that an individual cannot navigate one's journey of integrating one's Jewish identity with living in the world at large all by oneself. Each of us needs community, peers, friends, and teachers—and each of us needs a personal rabbi, a rebbe.

Accompanying me back from Jerusalem to college were my two new best friends: clarity and confusion. Both were ever present, both were strong and demanded attention, and both fed into each other. I vacillated in the course of a day, in the course of an hour, in the course of a moment, between the two. Each insight of clarity begat more confusion, and each moment of confusion begat more clarity. If anyone ever needed a rebbe, it was me. It was obvious I needed not only information, but guidance in how to decipher, interpret, and internalize it.

In reality, I even needed a rebbe to help teach me how to find a rebbe. My journey was in its embryonic stage. I recognized the need to turn to someone, wise and sensitive, to guide me as it birthed into infancy. However, the idea of "rabbi shopping" at different synagogues did not appeal to me. How would I even go about that anyway? Likewise, in 1971, the world was not yet filled to the brim with Chabad Houses, which would later serve as depots and transit centers for countless Jewish spiritual refugees who needed to feel welcomed into a world that was both alien and beckoning.

In an effort to connect with other Jews and miraculously meet my rebbe, I began to attend activities at the Hillel House. I also enrolled in Hebrew classes, as well as Jewish history and philosophy and anything else that the university offered about Israel and Judaism. An official Judaic Studies Department was not yet established, so the menu to choose from was sparse. However, this did not diminish the sense that I had found an oasis in the middle of a desert. This desert was not limited to the George Washington University campus, but rather included a harsh emptiness in my soul, barren of Jewish life and experiences. As King David writes in Psalms, "my soul thirsts for You; my flesh longs for you, in the dry and thirsty land, where there is no water" (Psalms 63:2).

My brain, transformed into a sponge, absorbed as much information as possible and as quickly as possible. I felt the deficit of not having been raised with a traditional Jewish education and upbringing and sensed an urgency to make up for lost time. Exhilarating as it was, this intense cerebral exercise brought with it more pain and disappointment.

Living in a world where I felt marginalized, as an outsider looking in, was not new to me. This was my "comfort zone" and quite familiar. However, this was the first time that I had desperately wanted to live in the world from which I was feeling so estranged. The Jewish world clearly grasped my attention and increasingly drew me closer and closer to its environs. However, while embracing the pull of generations, I could not ignore the feeling that if "they" knew the "real me," I would be denied entry. Never had I wanted to be a member in a club as much as now. Unfortunately, though, I had never felt as strongly as I did now that it would be almost impossible to join. However, I was determined to gain entry, one way or another, even at the cost of once again living a life that was not mine, but someone else's. I rationalized that I could live in the Jewish world as a man, and in the privacy of my heart and soul I would taste the joys of living in the same world as a female.

But I still needed a rebbe. I still inwardly heard this incessant voice directing me to find this unique individual who would "get me" and provide the guidance that I clearly needed.

And then it happened. I met him and knew; my soul cried with gratitude when he appeared. Unexpected, not forced nor contrived. I recall that day as if it were mere seconds ago. During fall semester 1971, the Hillel House distributed fliers advertising that a special rabbi would be teaching there on a certain Sunday afternoon. But he would not be teaching Judaic studies in a lecture hall, nor even in a small classroom. This rabbi taught in a style that was uniquely his. The flier advertised him as a "singing rabbi." The leaders at the Hillel House urged me to attend, cautioning me to arrive early as there could be hundreds of students showing up and of course I "needed" to be up front.

I anticipated the day with excitement and a sense that something important was about to happen. Something that might even resolve my inner conflict that never rested, even on Shabbat, the seventh day, the day of rest.

We were a group of no more than thirty eager souls, excited to share this new Jewish experience. None of us had any inkling of what was to occur at any moment. In walked a man whose presence immediately filled the room. He defined charisma. It was as if this warm ray of light entered and spread itself throughout the room. All I wanted to do was take shelter in his warmth and glow. His smile included everyone and yet seemed directed only at me. How could this be? A rabbi who looked like he was from Eastern Europe, from a different century, walked into my life, and for the first time, other than with my mother, I felt safe. He greeted us with incredible warmth by saying, "Shalom, holy brothers and sisters." No one had ever referred to me as holy—brother or sister! When he looked at me, all I could feel was that he connected to the deeper part of me, the part of me that transcended gender dysphoria and the confusion and pain it produced.

Oh, but this was just the beginning. He took out his guitar and began to sing, "The whole world is waiting to sing the song of Shabbos [Shabbat]." I had never heard these words, never heard this melody, never ever seen a rabbi with a long beard and a heavy Yiddish accent play a guitar and sing, encouraging all of us to sing along with him. What I heard was that the whole world was waiting for me to sing the song of Shabbos. For the first time in my life, I felt that my life really mattered, that just as I was, amid my utter confusion and pain, my life had intrinsic value and special, sacred worth. He made me feel precious and important, an importance neither egocentric nor one that would lead me to arrogance. Rather, I felt for the first time that I possessed the capacity to reach beyond my limited sense of self to an idea, to a belief, to values that were beyond the daily concerns of survival and consumption. All of this in the time it took for him to sing but the first few bars of music, the first melodic words of Torah.

I found myself crying tears of joy and gratitude. I had met my rebbe, the man whom I would learn to trust, to love, to respect, to learn from, and from whom I would receive guidance. I followed him over the next several decades, and regardless of where he saw me, in New York or in Israel, when he saw me he immediately acknowledged me by name with the same warmth and genuine care. In his unique nurturing way, he would hug me and ask how I was, always looking directly into my eyes. I sensed that he knew of my chronic suffering over my gender dysphoria. Yet somehow, when he hugged me and looked into my eyes, I actually believed that everything would be fine. In his presence I felt encouraged and safe. He gave me hope that a life dedicated to connecting to God as inspired in the holy Torah and being close to the real me and to the real others around me would be the way to achieve the inner healing that I so desperately sought.

Yes, meeting Rabbi Shlomo Carlebach on that November afternoon in 1971 changed my life forever. He openly welcomed me home into the club I thought would otherwise deny me entry. He welcomed me home—home, sweet home. My soul felt redeemed, revived, and refreshed

Chapter 7

WHAT A BEAUTIFUL WEDDING GOWN

In the spring of 1973, after graduating from college, I found myself standing under the chuppah, the wedding canopy under which a Jewish bride and groom stand as the rabbi officiates the wedding ceremony. As I stood under the chuppah, my two best friends, clarity and confusion, were right by my side.

I was clear that I felt a genuine, special love for the woman who was making her way to the chuppah to join me in marriage. But I was not feeling what I thought a groom should be feeling at this moment. I was clearly confused about what my love for this woman meant and what it signified. Intuitively I sensed that whatever loving feelings I had for her were not the typical feelings of a male groom toward his female bride. My deepest desire to see her happy propelled me to portray someone other than the real me.

My parents and grandparents were overjoyed. Their firstborn was getting married and honoring the age-old tradition of continuing the family line. This was what was expected of me, clearly and definitively. But it felt tragically wrong for me to be the groom in this time-honored tradition. How odd that I was the chatan, the groom, standing under the chuppah, waiting for his kallah, his bride, to join him. Shouldn't it have been a real man, a man who was sure of his masculinity, honestly and authentically standing under the chuppah waiting for me, his kallah, to join him? I couldn't help noticing the bride's beautiful wedding gown, and wishing I was the one wearing it.

She glided down the aisle with grace, with charm, and with a strength that was tempered yet evident. She proceeded with the joy of her childhood dreams coming true, with complete trust, love, commitment, and loyalty. The pure hopes for a wonderful future adorned her entire presence. Her own dreams and hopes personified everyone else's, as their gazing smiles accompanied her down the aisle. Everyone else's, that is, except mine.

I felt so incredibly guilty in this moment that I nearly ran away as fast as I could without ever looking back. This marriage was not fair to Susan, to our families, to our friends, to our community, and to the world, all because it was brutally unfair to myself. But I was held captive by the shackles of immense confusion and despair, paralyzing me from budging even an inch away from what was about to occur. I could not move, as I felt forced to live out someone else's dream, someone else's moment, and someone else's life. I felt my own sense of self disappear into the "other." This "other" within me stood there as the ceremony began. We left the chuppah as husband and wife, walking down the aisle amid cheers of joy. Everyone was smiling, and I myself managed to muster up the wherewithal to do the same. Inside, I was weeping, cringing in shame.

And so, the next phase of my deception began. Now the tentacles of my betrayal spread out beyond my family, my friends, and myself. I now betrayed the one individual in the world who had pledged her heart and soul to me. The one woman who desired to build a Jewish home and family with me was now stung by my pathetic inability to be honest and truthful. If anything was clear, it was this. If anything was confusing, it was not knowing what else to do.

CHAPTER 8

SIRENS ON YOM KIPPUR

In the summer of 1973, I returned to Israel. Landing at Ben Gurion Airport, I was filled with an immense sense of relief—as if I could breathe again. For two years I had longed to return. Not a day had passed since my first trip ended that I did not think of returning to Israel. I was growing into my Judaism, and Israel increasingly felt like home. As a budding avid Zionist, I knew that this was where I should be and where I would make my home. Of course, I had no idea how long it would take to accomplish my goal.

I deplaned with my wife as a newly married man. And I deplaned with heavy baggage: confusion and feelings of personal and global estrangement. I entered a country with no shortage of incredibly complex problems of her own, both domestic and international. And yet, I knew I had returned home. Israel's problems were my problems, in one way or another. My rebbe spoke frequently of Eretz Yisrael, the Land of Israel. He spoke with a reverence and love that affected me. Whenever Reb Shlomo, as his thousands of followers called him, mentioned the phrase "Eretz Yisrael," his eyes would light up even brighter than they usually did. Although he was physically in the United States, he spoke of Israel as if he were a stranger in a strange land, longing to return home. This certainty, this longing, was so powerful, so real, so true—so quintessentially "me."

And so I, too, left my familiar surroundings behind and came home. This time, my dream of working on a kibbutz came true. I made all the necessary arrangements in New York to ensure that my first home in Israel was Kibbutz Sdot Yam, the kibbutz on the beach that I had visited two years ago. Maybe there, I hoped, my soul would find respite.

While living on the kibbutz, I would visit Jerusalem from time to time. On each visit, as the bus climbed its final ascent toward the central bus station, my heart would skip a beat with excitement. The Holy City always welcomed me back home with open arms, embracing me at every step with no judgment.

A group of us Anglo volunteers decided we would observe Yom Kippur in Jerusalem. We overnighted at one of the hostels and looked forward to attending services the next day at the Western Wall.

Most Israelis do not observe Jewish practice in the way Orthodox tradition teaches. However, Yom Kippur in Jerusalem was unlike any other day of the year, and this was clear to everyone. As the sun was setting, ushering in the holiest day of the Jewish year, I felt immersed in the spiritual epicenter of the universe. An unfamiliar yet serene quietude fell upon Jerusalem as Jews from all over made their way to one of hundreds of various synagogues. All businesses and shops were closed. There was no traffic on the roads. People were dressed in white. Was I in heaven with the angels or on earth with human beings? Perhaps I was in both places at once.

On Yom Kippur, Jerusalem was in its splendor, absolutely magnificent. In a moment in time like this one, when I experienced my life through a spiritual lens, my own internal battle and chronic pain receded into a temporary state of latency. A stronger and greater force overpowered it, and for that not only was I grateful, but I easily surrendered to it when I felt its pull. Perhaps more than anything else, this was the experience that drew me inextricably to Jerusalem.

In the morning, our little group from the kibbutz made our way to the Kotel. I recall feeling protected and secure within this spiritual bubble of the Yom Kippur holiday in Jerusalem. I proceeded directly to the men's side, without thinking about my betrayal to myself. I knew that I belonged on the women's side. I also knew that I did not want to lose a moment of this spiritual relief and celebration by dwelling on my painful conflict.

Not knowing how to participate in the Yom Kippur prayer service with a minyan, a prayer quorum, I merely stood at the Wall by myself and offered my own prayers. I had not a clue what this most sacred day even meant. So, I prayed for world peace and for cures for the world's ailments. I also prayed, fervently, for an age in which people would accept one another's differences with kindness, an age devoid of mean-spirited dismissiveness.

My prayers came from my heart and were genuine. As my face was buried in the stones at the Wall, I meant what I said.

I expressed a real concern for conditions that desperately sought Divine attention and intervention. For me, doing anything that expressed the authentic me, whoever that person may have been, was my way of returning to God. And returning to God, as I learned later, is one of the main themes of Yom Kippur.

All of a sudden, and I mean suddenly, there were sirens ringing all around us, accompanied by loud announcements in garbled Hebrew. People started running, screaming, and crying. I had no idea what was going on. Our little group from the kibbutz quickly found one another. We agreed that if Israel were ever to be at war again, it would probably resemble this very scenario. However, it was Yom Kippur and no nation would ever dare attack another on its most holy day of the year—or so we thought! As it turned out, a coalition of Arab states led by Egypt and Syria did in fact attack Israel on the most holy day of the Jewish year. Hence, this surprise attack against Israel on October 6, 1973, became known as the Yom Kippur War.

I am not prone to being paranoid, but as we rushed out of the Old City through the Arab shuk (open market), I noticed the looks of glee and joy on many of the merchants' faces. I wish I could forget what this was like. Glee? Joy? Why? The Jewish people, making their way as quickly as possible out of the Old City, exhibited emotions ranging from extreme worry to complete panic. We made our way back to our hotel and soon realized that it would be impossible to return to the kibbutz until after the conclusion of the holiday at nightfall, war or no war, since the buses would not begin operating again until then. What we did not know, nor could we have known, was that the Israel Defense Forces (IDF) had immediately mobilized the stationed buses and used them to transport thousands of Israeli soldiers from their homes to their respective bases. It then became clear that returning to the kibbutz was going to be complex, to say the least. Oddly enough, despite finding myself in a war zone, I never felt that my life was in danger. This was due to either my naïveté or my absolute total trust in the IDF. Perhaps both.

As we made our way back to the kibbutz, the realities of a country at war quickly became apparent. The entire country was in blackout mode. Everyone had to hang blankets in their windows, preventing any light from illuminating the outside. In order to drive, you had to paint your headlights blue. Streetlights were turned off, rendering the roads as pitch black as possible.

One day earlier, our journey from the kibbutz to Jerusalem on two buses had lasted ninety minutes. That night, I lost count of how many buses we took before we actually returned to our home several hours later. Regular bus service was suspended, so we were completely dependent on any bus stopping for us and taking us as far as the driver's route would allow. The bus drivers were exhausted by nightfall after spending the better part of the holiday transporting soldiers to their bases.

We were grateful to be back safe and sound at the kibbutz, but over the next few days, two realities became quite apparent. First, it was essential that no volunteer leave. With just about all the men and many women of the community away at war, we volunteers became the backbone of the workforce for the kibbutz. The task of harvesting the cotton, a major profit-producing commodity for the kibbutz, was top priority. Once the rains began to fall, any unharvested cotton would be destroyed. Working twelve-hour days became the norm. Second, it seemed clear that Israel was losing the war.

Unlike the previous Six-Day War in 1967, which had brought a quick and undisputed victory, this would not be quick, and would take a heavy toll on the Israeli population.

Communicating with my parents during this time was extremely difficult. The kibbutz had only one phone that we volunteers could use for international calls. Due to the war, circuits were much busier than usual. Service worked intermittently at best. My parents wanted me on the next plane back to the United States. Ben Gurion Airport had been closed, but even if the airport had been operating, I would not, could not, leave. I would not leave the only place on earth where I felt at home. Safe or not, winning or losing, I was not budging. I felt the responsibility to work twelve-hour days harvesting the cotton for the kibbutz. I was needed! For the very first time in my life, I was actually needed to help do what is expected of one when one's home is under attack, and I felt it was the very least I could do.

Of course, there were times when I felt scared. At night, when the Israeli planes flew along the coast extremely low, so as to avoid being detected by Egyptian radar, our little one-room aluminum corrugated "house" would shake. Did I feel personally attacked? Of course. Would I leave my home when it was under attack? Absolutely not.

What's more, from the moment those sirens went off at the Western Wall, for the first time in twenty-two years I was not aware of my gender identity disorder. It was as if gender in all its significance was suspended for the time being. Gender had no relevance at the moment. We were one people who needed to unite to overcome a threat that had only one objective, the total annihilation of the Jewish homeland.

Miraculously, after the third day of fighting, the energy of the kibbutz shifted from doom and gloom to relief and gratitude. There was miraculous news! In less than a week, Israel had recovered and launched a strong counteroffensive. The IDF overtook both the Egyptian and Syrian forces, and victory was imminent.

After the war was over, I realized more than ever how extensive my gender identity disorder affected me and how incredibly pervasive it was. It took a national horrific calamity, a war, to take my mind off the subject. Temporarily, the war provided me relief from my all-encompassing issues. Ironically, it was a war that gave me an inkling of the peace that might be possible without the crippling and violent storm raging within me.

CHAPTER 9

ME? ORTHODOX? ME? A RELIGIOUS ZIONIST?

After the Yom Kippur War was over, I returned to the States to apply to graduate school. I knew when I was in college that I was meant to teach. This was my calling. I had to become an educator, and one of the best! This would be the one pursuit that would give value to my life. A life that severely lacked a sense of inner worth and self-esteem. I now needed to figure out what discipline within the vast field of education I would pursue.

At this time in my life, it became clear what my next step would be. I felt compelled to develop some workable expertise as a Judaic studies educator. Ready to plunge in headfirst, I applied to the master's program in Jewish education at the Jewish Theological Seminary of America (JTS).

Just a few years earlier, I had no sense of either a Jewish identity or an affinity with being a committed Zionist. Now I was resolving to teach others about both! What was I thinking? In truth, I wasn't thinking! I felt I had to do this. This decision came from my heart. It bypassed all objections, both from my own strong, ugly voice of gender dysphoria and from my parents, who did not restrain themselves from expressing their extremely strong opinions on the subject.

I was accepted to JTS and was pleasantly informed that all entering graduate students were required to spend the summer in Israel. And so, the summer of 1974 found me back in Israel again. This time it was not to tour, nor to work on a kibbutz, nor to do my part in helping the country during a war defending its very existence. It was now time to nurture my Jewish identity and career by delving into Judaic studies in earnest. I would immerse myself in the entire body of Judaic literature: the Bible, the Talmud, Jewish law, philosophy, history, mysticism, ethics, and the prolific body of rabbinic commentary, as well as biblical and rabbinic Hebrew and, to a degree, Aramaic. As the pull to integrate the traditional Jewish way of life into my general life became increasingly strong, this program seemed to be the perfect venue for creating the foundation for my teaching career.

In 1971, I felt relieved that my newly discovered pride in being Jewish in fact did not include religious observance. The Israelis I met espoused so much pride, so much commitment, and so much enthusiasm in being Israeli. Their Zionism did not include adherence to Jewish law, and yet, I sensed that they devoted their lives to a purpose greater than mere survival. Their understanding that each Israeli's life mattered captured my attention. That they were Jewish as well made this all the more comfortable and appealing, since for the first time I felt truly positive about being Jewish. But my newly acquired positivity about Judaism intertwined tightly with my newly discovered Zionist pride. The central role that Israel plays in the life of the Jew—the Jew from thousands of years ago, the Jew living today, the Jew living in Israel, and the Jew living in the Diaspora—began to play an increasingly central role in my own life.

The teachings from my rebbe, Rabbi Shlomo Carlebach, of blessed memory, echoed within me. His identity seemed at least as tied to Jewish spiritual tradition as any Israeli's identity was bound to the physical Land of Israel. I found myself at a crossroads. I was not my rebbe, and I was not a modern Israeli. I didn't know who I was.

I did not grow up in a traditional Orthodox observant home. I did not grow up in Israel. But now I was faced with a startling reality. As my Zionist leanings grew, so did my interest in Judaism. As I inquired what Jewish traditional living meant to me, my Zionist inclinations grew stronger and stronger. It was becoming increasingly difficult to keep the two distinctive entities separate in my head. Soon, it would become impossible to separate the two in my heart.

Only one person supported me. The one person whom this decision would affect, next to me, the most. My wife. The more she supported me, the worse I felt inside for not being honest with her about my inner demons. I was filled with fear that she would leave me if she knew. I wanted to leave me for knowing about me, so I projected that feeling onto everyone else I knew, especially my loved ones.

Back in Jerusalem for the summer, an amazing surprise awaited me. All the emotion that my rebbe awoke in my heart, Torah learning awoke in my brain. I loved, loved, loved learning biblical passages with commentaries, learning about Shabbat and the festivals, studying the Hebrew language, and learning the history of Israel.

With passion and vigor I began to partake of these wellsprings of wisdom in the Jewish tradition, passed down from generation to generation over several millennia. I drank like someone who was painfully parched with thirst in a desert. I ate like someone who was ravenous with hunger. Each of my teachers, while different, was the same. How they taught expressed their individuality. What they taught expressed their common pride, passion, and commitment to furthering the Jewish tradition to the next generation—to the next generation of Jewish educators.

I began observing some aspects of Shabbat, the Sabbath. Without consciously making a decision to do so, I started keeping kosher, adhering to the Torah-defined dietary laws. I started attending prayer services. I became more comfortable reading Hebrew and even speaking a little. I began understanding more and more of my people's language, and was stimulated by it more than I had ever been by my native English. The more I immersed myself, the more I wanted. If only, if only this immersion had miraculously rid me of my inner demon of disconnect between my body and soul. Perhaps, I told myself, it would in time.

My fellow students and I engaged in discussions that revolved around matters of the spirit, rather than matters of the body. These invigorated and refreshed me. The need to understand and find one's place within the tapestry of Jewish community arose in almost every discussion. The desire grew daily.

My own connection between everything I learned and the place in which I was learning strengthened my desire, my need, and my resolve to move to Israel. The idea of living in Israel began to feel natural, not like moving to a foreign country.

I continually found myself at the Western Wall. Each time I went to the Wall, I experienced the charade of approaching the epicenter of Jewish spirituality in disguise. I knew this was not sustainable. This charade extended far beyond my physical approach to the holy site. It infected my soul. My very soul, which so eagerly began to immerse itself in Jewish tradition and in Jerusalem, was betrayed by a force that felt utterly beyond my control. It was a wild demon within me that sought to sabotage all my efforts to connect with my spiritual center, with God, with my fellow Jewish brothers and sisters, and with all of humankind. This tension could not, would not, be sustainable.

I halfheartedly returned to New York to attend JTS at the end of the summer—wondering. Was I becoming Orthodox? A religious Zionist? These were labels among the Jewish people that for the first twenty-two years of my life represented everything I wanted to avoid. Now they had evolved into a way of life that I wanted to run toward. But I kept asking myself: "Me? Orthodox? Me? A religious Zionist? Me? Both?" These questions, different and yet the same, boarded the flight with me back to the States and became louder and louder with every passing day. The answer simultaneously became clearer and more confusing: Yes, but how? Of course, but of course not. Absolutely, and absolutely not!

Chapter 10

BUT WHAT ABOUT GOD?

Back in Manhattan after my third trip to Israel, I began my master's degree program in Jewish education at JTS in the fall of 1974. Feeling inspired and enthusiastic to learn more of my heritage, my people's language and history, I was compelled to grapple with the unique, odd puzzle that has puzzled historians, philosophers, and anthropologists for centuries: the Jewish people. More than my intellectual drive, though, my awakening spirituality filled my life with a new purpose, a new love. Atrophied until now, my tormented, confused, fragmented, and broken soul was coming to life, beckoning me to overcome the cause of its hurt. The reality of HaShem was increasingly on my mind.

I entered each new class with vigor and hope. Every day was a fresh chance to encounter HaShem through text, language, commentaries, group discussions, and inquiry. I believed that the "theories of education" classes I attended and my rigorous research of pedagogical practices would enrich my understanding of how to transmit Jewish tradition to the next generation. With an open mind and heart, I welcomed the opportunity to learn about the secret ingredient to the Jewish people's miraculous survival—and how to share that with my future students.

And beyond the walls of the seminary, I never despaired that this would somehow, some way be my ticket home to myself, resolving the never-ending, gnawing pain that threatened any hope to do so. I imagined that the real remedy for what ailed me would be found by cultivating a real relationship with God.

While still in Jerusalem, a few weeks before I returned to New York, one of my colleagues in the summer learning program cautioned me. Out of concern for me, he reminded me that Manhattan is not Jerusalem and that the professors at JTS are not the rabbis that shared their love of learning Torah and knowledge with us during the summer. The challenge in Jerusalem was to apply HaShem's message by living a life permeated with spiritual expression. The challenge at JTS, he warned, would be to figure out my appreciation of text through critical thinking. The approach in Jerusalem fed my soul. The approach at JTS would be cerebral calisthenics.

I dismissed his words, not wanting to believe them. I loved the summer learning program and looked forward to it continuing in New York. I would not believe anything to the contrary, even though in an eerie way I sensed he knew what he was talking about.

After one week of classes, I became despondent. Why didn't these professors talk about HaShem? Why didn't they discuss the condition of the soul? Why did they approach what I believed to be sacred texts with academic arrogance and sarcasm? These scholars, whom I looked up to, who I hoped would inspire me to explore with even more diligence and passion, seemed so sure of themselves. It appeared that we were not on a joint venture of discovery, but rather on one of joint criticism.

The "theories of education" classes I took elevated modern pedagogy to a "holier than thou" ordained status, reducing thousands of years of scholarship to the simplistic and irrelevant. This abrasive attitude and lack of basic respect toward traditional Jewish insights on education was more than offensive. I was bewildered, shocked, and disappointed. My colleague in Jerusalem was right. Too right.

In the world of graduate studies, JTS exemplified an academically rigorous institution of the highest caliber. Intellectually, I was incredibly stimulated and challenged. For this I remained grateful. However, I did not enroll as a student to only be academically challenged. I made the choice to attend JTS to also explore, consider, and contemplate the presence of God in my life.

But what about God? Was God to be found within the walls of JTS? Where did God go? Did the Divine spirit, HaShem, remain in Jerusalem? If so, I belonged there, and clearly not at JTS in New York.

To my pleasant and unexpected surprise, I did eventually find God at JTS. Not in the classroom, but rather in fellow students and in one person in particular.

In my classes I never hesitated to challenge the arrogant tone of my professors, who dismissed the presence of God in modern Judaic living as cute and unsophisticated. I felt hurt and angry. I felt that magic cure-all to gender dysphoria slipping out of my grasp. I felt that my soul was drying up, denied its nourishment, deprived of the nurturing that was critical for its well-being. So, I lashed out at my professors. How dare they imply that leaving God out of biblical scholarly inquiry is Jewish! Greek it may be, modern it may be, Western it may be—but Jewish, of course not.

A colleague of mine encouraged me to attend an informal class that met weekly in one of the dorm rooms. The class was about being in relationship with HaShem. The teacher discussed how to live with the tension of one's essence, one's soul, inhabiting a physical body, each one crying out with its own needs to flourish and demanding attention. How does one create a balance between these two centers of energy? Wow! How could I say no? Why would I say no? This was the class I had incessantly sought.

That first night, I walked into the designated room and joined a group of about ten students. The young man who was teaching looked radically different from the rest of us. No jeans, no T-shirt or flannel shirt, no sandals or running shoes. In stark contrast, he wore a suit and white shirt, sporting a scraggly untrimmed beard with a black fedora perched on his head. He could not have been a day older than me, perhaps even younger. However, he appeared to have been transported in a time machine from a different time and place. He reminded me of some of the ultra-Orthodox Chassidic Jewish men I saw in Jerusalem.

Immediately I could sense myself moving along a spectrum from one extreme to the other. One part of me wanted to leave before it was too late, and the other part wanted to stay, just out of curiosity. I did not have to struggle with what to decide, since as soon as he saw me, he welcomed me with the warmest greeting, "Shalom," followed by one of the most genuine handshakes I ever recall experiencing. He even appeared grateful to meet me, to greet me, and to include me. Yossi then began to teach from a book, written in Hebrew. Those who attended regularly had their own copies. They eagerly followed along with him—their eyes moving on the page with excitement.

I did not understand a word he said. I was unable to follow the Hebrew in the copy he lent me. I am not even sure I knew what point he was making. However, I heard the word HaShem repeated several times throughout the one-hour lesson. I saw passion in his eyes, and beyond. In his voice, I sensed the love of God and of the text. I felt how important it was to him that each student in the room felt comfortable with the text and connected with it. I shared a moment of text study with a person who is devoted. A young man whose commitment to living included connecting with that Being who was, is, and always will be infinitely greater than the sum total of creation.

In one hour, this person taught me more about the sacredness of Jewish text than all of my professors combined in all the time I had been at JTS for the past several weeks. In one hour, this teacher taught me how I would one day teach my own students!

All I could say at the end of this pivotal moment in my journey was "What is the name of this book?" and "I'm in. Can you please bring me a copy next week?" His answer, with a smile, was "Tanya, and with God's help, yes."

But what about God? We found each other here in a dorm room at JTS in a text referred to as Tanya taught by this incredible rabbi-in-training named Yossi. Now I found hope again to heal, to be normal, to push this horrific conflict out of my heart and soul, once and for all!

Chapter 11

IN LEAH'S KITCHEN

Moving further and further into the world of Orthodox Jewry, I continued studying at JTS but found spiritual fulfillment elsewhere. Learning Tanya with Yossi both answered old questions and raised new ones. I appreciated the need to acquire a master's degree to advance my career in Jewish education. However, I appreciated even more the teachings in Tanya. The wisdom in this book inspired my spiritual quest to connect with God, my soul, and my Jewish tradition. Focusing on my spiritual journey now included paying more attention to my observance of Jewish law. This left mercifully little room to negotiate with my inner demons.

I began living as if these dark forces no longer existed. I convinced myself that my commitment to Jewish tradition somehow expunged them. I turned my back on them and denied their presence in my life. I was on to something important—something big. I would not let anyone or anything stop me from exploring this uncharted territory. In one breath I both embraced and denied what mattered to me the most—the truth. One Friday evening I entered the main Chabad-Lubavitch synagogue in Crown Heights, Brooklyn, world headquarters of Rabbi Menachem Mendel Schneerson, the spiritual leader of this Chassidic dynasty. Yossi was a Lubavitcher chassid, a follower of "the Rebbe," as he was referred to by the thousands of his followers across the globe.

When he invited me to spend Shabbat in this part of New York, I had little idea what I would experience. To some the neighborhood appears rundown, aging without grace, a hotbed of racial tension between those who wear black and those who are black. A far cry from the vibrancy and magical energy I connected with in Jerusalem. Yet, to those who made their home in this Brooklyn neighborhood, Crown Heights was everything Jerusalem represented, and perhaps even more.

Immediately I felt as if I were swimming in a sea of black—black hats, black suits, black coats, black shoes, black beards. I was a stranger here. I told myself I did not belong here. I told myself I'd gone too far. I told myself that all I wanted to do, all I was passionate about, was to celebrate my Jewish identity—with the undying hope that somehow this would provide me with the healing I desperately sought from my own inner brokenness. Chassidic Jews? Living in an old, tired, forgotten, and even dangerous part of Brooklyn? And the black—wherever I turned—so much black! Why? I wanted to see the world in living color with all its diverse shades and permutations.

And yet, something powerful called to me during my first visit to what I thought was no-man's-land: community, passion, commitment to high ideals, hope for a better world, enthusiasm about being Jewish, and even a deep gratitude for having been born a Jew. I saw this in everyone's eyes. I felt it. Yet, when entering the synagogue for the Friday night Shabbat prayers, I felt like an outsider gazing through the peephole. I convinced myself that if they knew the real me, I surely would have been denied entry.

So there I was, swimming in my personal "Black Sea." A dark, murky, cold Black Sea.

As in Jerusalem, the men assembled in one designated area, and the women in another. Once again I had to decide. But unlike that first time at the Western Wall, I really didn't have to decide. Drowning in the awful quicksand of denial, pulling me further down, without missing a beat, I dove into the men's section of the Black Sea.

I could not wait to leave. The smells, the voices, the bodies, the energy reeked of masculinity. This was just like being in a men's locker room, the secret clubhouse I dreaded entering when younger. And here I was again—once again in the bastion of unbridled, abrasive, brotherly male energy. But where was my place? I gazed up at the women's section above. I envied my wife, who was so fortunate to be where she knew she belonged—in the women's locker room.

Suddenly, he appeared. Everyone aggressively whispered, "Shush, shush, shush." Throngs of people moved back, creating a temporary path, reminiscent of the parting of the Sea of Reeds when the newly freed Children of Israel left Egypt. The Lubavitcher Rebbe entered the synagogue, and all eyes followed his every move. Incredible! Never have I seen one person command such devoted attention by his mere presence. OK, I told myself. I will stay. I must stay.

Despite these grand beginnings, to my utter disappointment, I did not witness anything spectacular. The Friday evening prayers began without ceremony. The Rebbe sat in his designated place of honor in front of everyone, sometimes rising, appearing to pray along with everyone else. He was not even the one who led the service. At the conclusion of the service, I witnessed once again the splitting of the sea. The Rebbe gently made his way through, wishing everyone a "gut Shabbos" as he departed. The throngs of worshippers, husbands, fathers with their sons in tow, little toddlers, brothers, grandfathers, single men from all over the world—and me—exited the synagogue to meet their female counterparts, families, and friends. Walking with my host family to their home for the special Shabbat dinner, I hear myself repeating the same question over and over: "What was that about?"

At the conclusion of the Sabbath on Saturday night, my hosts urged me to stay the night and wait until Sunday morning to return back to my apartment in Manhattan. Their urgings conveyed so much genuine intent. They really wanted their guests to remain. So, we did.

On Sunday morning I reflected on the weekend. I experienced multi-generational families with their guests, sitting around a big table together, eating and drinking sumptuous meals. No one rushing to finish, no one leaving to go somewhere else—everyone seemed to be exactly where they were meant to be, where they wanted to be. I witnessed everyone joyously singing time-honored Jewish songs at the table, engaging in lively discussions about the Bible and HaShem. Different people quoted the Rebbe's insights on how to connect with our spiritual center, our soul. I heard the word HaShem, over and over. Baruch HaShem—thank God. B'Ezrat HaShem—with the help of God. Chas V'Shalom—God forbid.

This was a deeper dimension of any Shabbat I had yet to experience, including when I was in Jerusalem. These people wanted to be with one another, and they wanted to talk about God in their lives. Five-year-olds, teenagers, adults, and grandparents.

I was shaken up. I wanted this, and yet, I didn't. I was caught between two opposing forces—pristine clarity and incredible confusion. I paced inside my head: "If I don't leave now, I may stay. But if I stay, I have no place. But if I leave, I will regret it. But if I stay, I won't know where to go." I exhausted myself going back and forth between the black and white of this world. After all, I lived in a world that was anything but black and white. Oh, how a part of me so longed to live in a world where everything seemed to make sense. Everything had an answer. Every imaginable aspect of human behavior was either allowed or forbidden.

In my own desperation to experience some kind of inner tranquility, I actually believed that this was how Orthodox Jews live. I wanted to believe, and so I did, that all Orthodox Jews were the collective expression of one individual. One individual living in God's imaginary paradise on earth. But how could I have known better?

At breakfast, Mordechai, the head of the family, left to take care of errands. The boys left the breakfast table to go to yeshiva—the traditional Jewish school teaching biblical studies. So, who remained? Sitting at the table was Leah, Mordechai's wife—the architect, the engineer, the producer, the powerhouse, the artist, the chef, the queen bee in this beautiful home—who so generously and warmly hosted me. With Leah were her daughters, my wife—and me. Once again, "and me." We talked, and talked, and talked over refill after refill of delicious freshly brewed coffee.

Then I knew. Clarity without confusion. I knew where I belonged. Not swimming in the Black Sea. Not in the men's locker room. Not in the all-male yeshiva. I belonged with other women, in Leah's kitchen! Being with Leah—experiencing her spark, her spunk, her intellect, the ease with which she flowed from discussing the weekly Torah portion and God's presence in the world in one breath to where she had bought her new dress in the next, her patience with her children, her joy in doing everything imaginable to make me feel comfortable—this was the ideal life for me.

And yet, I knew if I didn't leave right then I would never be able to sustain this masquerade. That thought petrified me, urged me to get up, leave, and never turn back. But I did not. I surrendered to the truth, to the inclination to remain right where I was, in Leah's kitchen. Leah said nothing to me that implied I did not belong at the table with all the women. This in and of itself was strange against the backdrop of such a binary gender-defined and -separated community. I effortlessly discovered a piece of my warm soul on a bitterly cold winter morning in Crown Heights, Brooklyn—in Leah's kitchen. So, why leave?

Chapter 12

SOUL TRANSPLANT

I lived in Crown Heights from 1976 to 1977, succumbing to incredible pressure. There was horrendous pressure from within me to fit in, and never-ending pressure outside me to do the same. For many reasons, I never mustered up enough courage to challenge either myself or anyone else. I felt I had no right to question. I moved to the epicenter of the Chabad-Lubavitch world to calm the waters within myself, and instead they became more turbulent. I felt I was being sucked into a life that was more about looking and speaking the part assigned to me than about discovering my unique place. But then again, in 1976, would that have even been possible? I convinced myself that if I went along with the incessant demands made on me, God would reward me with living a somewhat normal life—having not a clue what normalcy meant.

So, as I entered a community steeped in sacred tradition, I pathetically capitulated, never feeling that anything I did was enough. I started observing Jewish law on the strictest level imaginable, which in and of itself was not problematic. The problem was that I did this all in a disguise. I parroted back the lines fed to me. I mimicked everyone around me. I even began to dress like I had just immigrated from pre-Holocaust Russia.

The day I put on a black fedora and long black coat, the day I stopped shaving my facial hair to grow out a beard, was one of the saddest days I can remember. I looked in the mirror, and all I could think was "What have I become?" Living a life of piety? Of truth? Of spirituality? Of God's will for me? Not for a second did I fool myself into believing such lies. Here I was, a woman on the inside, held hostage by her male body, living a lie dedicated to living the life of absolute truth. The only way I could survive this was to plunge even deeper into my Black Sea and surrender out of desperation to honor something worthwhile. There was always a stricter level of observance to reach, and tragically I felt only increasing lack. But I yearned to matter, to be counted, to be a member, even at the expense of my very integrity.

I envied everything my wife did as an ultra-Orthodox Chassidic woman. I lived vicariously through her and her girlfriends. Everything I learned in this community about the way traditional Judaism views the essential spiritual differences between a man and a woman only made it worse for me. Very little about the male role in a traditional Jewish community resonated with me. Almost everything about the female role did.

I never really understood how all the men with whom I was forced to socialize thought and communicated. All efforts to connect with them exhausted me. I never "got them." When I was able to "sneak" around the women, I felt such relief. Effortlessly, I understood their language. Not so much in a cerebral way, but in an intuitive experiential way. I made no real "guy" friends. I lived the life of a fraud, immersed in a pool of passionate commitment to living the truth.

I began to realize that the honor shown to the Lubavitcher Rebbe resulted from his unique way of approaching God, fellow Jews, and all of humanity—with love, patience, and humility—always giving others the benefit of the doubt. Like his other followers, I began to quote his teachings in every crevice of my life. What drew me to this amazing man was his undying commitment to infuse the world with kindness and goodness. The Lubavitcher Rebbe dedicated his life of service to God with a sense of uncompromising urgency and love. He lived a life clearly focused on bringing redemption: personal redemption, community redemption, Jewish nationhood redemption, and universal redemption for all humankind as prophesied by the classical prophets in the Bible.

I thought that being a follower of the Lubavitcher Rebbe would provide me with my own channel to personal redemption. After all, how could he be wrong? He quoted God's text with ease and with unwavering belief and loyalty to its Divine origin. The population of his followers began to swell. Jewish people the world over started moving into Crown Heights. His presence as a righteous, holy man became evident in Israel by both religious and nonobservant Israelis. World leaders, in both the Jewish and non-Jewish worlds, would seek out the Rebbe's wise counsel and advice.

While living in the Crown Heights community pushed me further and further into deceptive living, the Rebbe himself drew me closer and closer to developing my own authentic relationship with God. At the same time, Reb Shlomo Carlebach, whose music and teachings continued to bring tears to my eyes, remained a steadfast, strong influence in my life as well. Both of my rebbes taught me the same lessons: Connect with yourself, all Jews, and all fellow human beings; be honest, be vulnerable, be loving, be in relationship with your soul and everyone else's, be true to being you! Ultimately this would lead to sensing God's presence in every facet and expression of creation. All I could do with this knowledge was sigh.

While living in Brooklyn and finishing up my master's degree at JTS, dressed now like my teacher Yossi, I became a father for the first time. I helped bring a healthy, lively, beautiful boy into the world. His birth filled me with immense gratitude, joy, and celebration. His birth also filled me with even more confusion. If I couldn't be an honest man, an honest Jewish man, an honest religious Jewish man, an honest religious Jewish husband, then how could I be the father that this newly revealed miracle deserved? At this point all I wanted, all I begged for, all I pleaded for was to miraculously become the man that my body messaged I was supposed to be.

I needed a soul transplant. That would fix me. With a new soul, I could become the ideal husband for the woman I loved, and then become the best father possible for our son. "I will," I repeated to myself. I will. But how? How does one become someone else? I had no idea. That chapter was somehow omitted in the Jewish texts I had studied until now. The great sages and rabbis left that out of the curriculum or, at the very least, it was a tightly guarded secret.

So, my lie continued and worsened. I would have surrendered my life in a flash to spare my infant son the least bit of harm, and yet, I could not live my life honestly as a testimony to my unconditional love for him. I felt so protective of him. Yet, how I lived my inner life denied him the fatherly, male nurturing that he rightfully needed, and would grow to expect. A right that he had inherited simply by being my son, by virtue of the fact that I was his father.

So, where does a Jew go for a soul transplant? To the one place that revealed Jewish mysticism to the world, the language of the soul, the deepest spiritual teachings. With my wife, our one-year-old safely snuggled in my arms, and my master's degree in hand, I moved to the enchanting little city of Tzfat, Israel, in Upper Galilee. This is where I would undergo my soul transplant.

Chapter 13

PUNISHING THE CHILD FOR THE PARENT'S SIN

From the summer of 1977 to 1979, I lived a dreamlike life in Tzfat. I walked in the shadows of the most revered Jewish mystics. I occupied space inhabited by the most holy men and women who preceded my existence by several centuries. I lived with people who exemplified the uncompromising commitment to living a life of truth, to honoring one's soul, and to dedicating one's efforts to serving the Divine.

And then there was me. What a contrast! What a contemptible contrast. Outwardly I appeared like any other Chassidic male. However, I cringed each time I fulfilled the daily rituals traditionally observed by men alone. This self-contempt remained a tightly guarded secret between God and me.

Observing how my wife cared for our first child, and watching her experience a second pregnancy, almost drove me to the brink of spiritual suicide. I would have done anything, absolutely anything, to have been assigned her role in the Jewish community. How I envied her! This envy chipped away, day by day, at the little integrity I had managed to build by living a spiritual life anchored in Jewish tradition, until one day God answered my prayers—if only partially.

I was allowed a glimpse into the world of which I yearned to be a part. The world of which I was meant to be a part. Miraculously, and for me this was indeed a miracle, I received a teaching position in an all-girls religious high school. Aside from the head of school, I was considered to be the only man on the staff. Aside from the head of school, I considered there to be no other males on the staff. Immersion in an all-female environment afforded my soul respite. I could breathe; I was alive, more true to myself than ever before. And again, these elated feelings remained a carefully guarded secret between God and me. No one else was privy to dwell with me in my inner chamber of relief, a concealed space that was clean, honest, and authentic. How invigorating! I intermingled with all my female colleagues and students seamlessly. More often than not I forgot my soul was hidden in a male body. It was the closest I had ever come to living a life of truth.

So, when asked how I liked my work, I would immediately reply without a moment's hesitation. I loved it, absolutely loved it! And that was the most honest statement I could have made. It felt odd, and yet so wonderful, to be truthful with others. Those were rare moments, worthy of inner celebration.

The irony of this situation was not lost on me. For the first time in my life, I was immersed in an all-female environment. For the first time in my life, my female self felt safe and found expression. I felt invigorated. I felt normal. All the while living in one of the most Orthodox Chassidic centers in Israel, in one of the most gender-separated communities imaginable.

Here, of all places, HaShem blessed me with compassion and love.

Unexpectedly, this attempt at living happily ever after to the best I could manage came to a screeching halt. Abruptly, everything changed. In the course of one day, "living the life" ceased to be. Due to a serious health condition with my second child, I painfully realized that I had to move my family back to the United States.

In a way, I went into spiritual shock. Circumstances beyond my control forced me to bid farewell to the home—both physical and spiritual—I had finally found. My religious Zionist identity cried out in agony. The thought of having to leave Israel horrified me. Even worse, I needed to stop teaching. To ensure the financial means necessary to properly care for my child's special needs, I made the painful decision to work for my father, where I could earn a better wage. This meant leaving the all-female environment and entering a business that catered to an all-male, blue-collar customer base. As if that were not enough, the thought of having to return to the place of my childhood petrified me. That place may have been ideal for my sisters to have grown up in, but for me it was a nightmare. As far back as I could remember, going to school and camp meant being the brunt of jokes by "the guys" for being, walking, talking, and behaving "just like a girl."

This had to be a judgment executed only by the Divine court above. This defined punishment in every understanding of the word. I had been expelled from heaven, torpedoing straight into hell at the speed of lightning.

I remembered having learned the verse in the Bible about God visiting the iniquity of the parents upon the children and grandchildren. I convinced myself that my innocent little baby daughter's condition was God's way of punishing me for not being honest. I was being punished for outwardly and deceptively portraying myself as male, when I'd always known that I was female.

It was I who was guilty of fraud, and yet, all of us—my wife, our two children, and I—were punished. Forced to leave the holy city of Tzfat and the holy Land of Israel, we were sent back into exile, into the Diaspora, to live among the nations of the world. We were uprooted from the soil indigenous to nurturing our Jewish identity. Banished to living on foreign soil as strangers in a strange land. I was convinced that my pathetic inability to live a life of authenticity had brought this on.

Of course, I had to provide the necessary resources for my daughter's educational and medical needs. That was never in doubt or negotiable. But I convinced myself that I knew what lay underneath this unfortunate situation. The foundation of living a Jewish life, raising a Jewish family, and living the Zionist dream crumbled before me. This tore me to pieces inside. Any guilt I had previously experienced paled in comparison to what I now felt.

In just two years, so much had changed. My move to Israel in 1977 brought me home. The decision to move there was one of the few I ever made based in truth. With it I felt a deep commitment to my Jewish identity, to my family, to my people—and to God. Leaving Israel in 1979 brought me back to exile. Whatever truth I held on to crumbled before me. With my head up, I arrived, and with my head down, I left.

But why? Why would my daughter and, by extension, my family suffer this punishment? Why does God visit the iniquity of the parents on the children? Why does God punish the child for the parent's sin? Many years passed before I began to understand what this really meant. For now I took it literally, and consequently was plagued with even more guilt and more questions than answers.

PART TWO

LIVING IN FEAR AND SHAME 1979–1985

Chapter 14

FROM THE PAN TO THE FIRE

The transition between the last week of June 1979 in Tzfat and the first week of July in Patchogue, New York, resembled a Kafkaesque-Felliniesque movie script: complex, illogical, and bizarre. It was an intellectual nightmare and an emotional trauma. Life as I knew it came to a screeching halt. This, combined with the gnawing feelings of guilt, plagued me daily.

I was outwardly living as a Chassidic male, working with my father in the very town where I grew up. This period of time was excruciating from every vantage point imaginable. I was an Orthodox Jew in an un-Orthodox area, with a growing family, having been uprooted from the country I felt to be my home. I was confronted with haunting memories from my tormented childhood. As if this weren't enough, my gender dysphoria became increasingly pronounced, regardless of the strict Chassidic Orthodox Jewish lifestyle I had adopted.

These six long years working in a predominantly male, blue-collar environment caused me to live in fear and shame. I was petrified that one day I would simply snap, unable to maintain this charade one moment longer. I lived in shame for being so obsessed with my inner turmoil. This anxious misery fed on itself like a tumorous cancer, and significantly handicapped my ability to be the ideal husband and loving father I strove to be.

While of course I never received the "soul transplant" I so desired, and while my inner demons certainly followed me to Tzfat, I had maintained a certain level of tranquility in Israel. It was comforting to know that at least a part of me authentically honored some of my core values. I fervently believed that as a religious Zionist, the ideal place to raise my children was in Israel. They would benefit by growing up in Israel in ways unattainable in the Diaspora, even in the finest Jewish communities. In Israel, Jewish families experienced continuity and stability, successfully transmitting the Jewish spiritual and cultural values to the next generation without the same obstacles they would have faced in the Diaspora.

Now the tides had turned and washed me up on the shores of Long Island, reliving the embarrassment, humiliation, and hurt of my childhood. At eighteen, I had left this town, never intending to look back. Ten years later, I felt forced to return to help care for my daughter and her significant medical needs. As a loving, responsible parent, I made the right choice, but it was mixed with so much brokenness. All I could do was immerse myself in any and all efforts necessary to ensure her the finest resources available. This is what good parents do, and this is what I did.

But my assurance that I'd made the "right" decision did not help me sleep at night or feel comfortable in my daily life.

On one hand, I felt betrayed by the God I professed to worship. Yet, I believed that my own choice to be dishonest caused this painful scenario in my life. Consequently, I never once thought to give up and leave my efforts to live a life based on traditional Judaism. I surrendered to the reality that I would always be challenged by my own Judaism, even more than the world in general, to live an authentic life. My return to New York was spiritually and emotionally crippling. Now not only did I have my constant struggle of gender identity, but the ease with which I was able to express my religious spirituality in Israel was now removed, and I had to struggle on that end as well.

Day after day I woke up in the morning feeling disappointment. In Tzfat, the air was fresh and clean. Each time I entered the Old City, I walked back in time to an era in which people honored their souls at any and every cost. Nothing in the world as I knew it from birth could compete with this commitment. After two years immersed in this enchanting environment, being on Long Island was depressing.

I made a promise to myself that as soon as humanly possible I would move back to Israel, this time to Jerusalem. In Jerusalem, I would find all the resources my daughter needed to ensure her well-being. In Jerusalem, I would finally find myself at home.

But for now I was not home. For now I was roasting in the flames of hell—and it hurt, it hurt terribly!

Chapter 15

IN HIDING

The Dark Ages of my life span the years 1979–1985. Stunted, trapped, invisible, I sense that I am disintegrating into a corpse: barely breathing, barely alive, and barely thinking or feeling.

On July 3, 1981, I wake up to my thirtieth birthday stressed, exhausted, deflated. I wake up to this nightmare of reality every day. I ask myself, "Why is this day different than any other day?" I answer, "It isn't." I ask myself, "Am I really in Patchogue? Why am I not waking up in Israel? Is this really my life?" I recall how ten years earlier I celebrated my twentieth birthday on my first visit to Israel. Why is this day different than any other day? Today, on my thirtieth birthday, I am more aware than ever before of my own suffering.

Each morning when I realize I am awake, as I observe the Jewish tradition, I utter a statement of thanksgiving to God for the blessing of waking up to another day of life. The very first words a Jew utters, while still in bed, are "modeh ahni"—I thank you. Each morning I somehow muster up the wherewithal to utter modeh ahni. The very first two-syllable word that my breath releases into the world each morning belies the truth. My life is a curse. Even grammar betrays me. The Hebrew language is gender defined. So, not only am I saying "modeh," thank you, and not meaning it, I am using the masculine form of the verb, and not "modah," in the feminine. Even my lie is lying. While my lack of thankfulness is the essence of the lie, even the way I express it is not in truth.

I imagine what my life would be like if I could say modah ahni and mean it. I imagine what miracle it would take for me to wake up feeling grateful for the blessing of life, rather than cursed. I imagine waking up so grateful that my very first words would be to simply say to my Creator, "thank You," and to really mean it! Impossible!

And I know. I know exactly what my life would have to be like for that to happen, and I also know that I might as well dream to sprout wings and soar upward into the sky. In those years, the reality that my body could actually become that of a woman, literally, totally evaded me. I had no idea that as a caterpillar, entrapped in my own skin, I could indeed undergo a metamorphosis and emerge into a butterfly.

So, I wake up in hiding, I go through the motions of the day in hiding, and I go to sleep in hiding. I am petrified that someone will find out who I really am. After all, I myself am petrified of who I really am!

As I live a life in hiding, I adopt a survival mentality, clutching my deception with desperation. As a drowning victim pitifully seeks salvation in a little piece of floating driftwood, I frantically hold on to something false as well. I live in the singular "I" and "me." Even with a growing family, living in a community with other traditional Jews, the mental space of "us" and "we" remains foreign.

Running, running, running. I am always running, always in hiding—from myself, from the truth, from reality. I become a refugee—wounded, broken, and hurting, fleeing my oppressive forces. Always looking behind me, always afraid. I convince myself that I am a victim of circumstance. But I have no time to feel sorry for myself. I am too busy, too consumed, too immersed in simply getting through the day, hour by languishing hour. I violate whatever sense of self I once had. I wonder if I actually have any sense of self left at all.

Chapter 16

MEETING AND EXCEEDING EXPECTATIONS

During these six years, the Dark Ages of my life, no one had a clue that I was in hiding. How could they? Why would they? Outwardly I went through my day as expected, never expressing my true feelings. I basically lived in autopilot mode, neither thinking nor feeling. I became an expert in betrayal—I betrayed myself, my God, and my family. While my spiritual and emotional life went unattended, I overcompensated by constantly meeting the expectations of my daily life and at times even exceeding them. I became anxious at the mere thought of failing to perform as trained. I became devoted to pleasing others.

I wore many hats and wore them all well. I played the role of a devoted husband, father, son, community member, and

Chabad-Lubavitcher chassid—all externally, all in the guise of a shell that concealed my broken state of being. However, as much as I tried, and I tried hard, there was simply no escaping myself.

I did everything possible to ensure my wife all the physical comforts she needed and wanted, even comforts she herself never asked for. Nothing she needed or wanted was ever too much. And nothing I did for her left me feeling that it was enough. We bought a beautiful house with enough bedrooms, bathrooms, and comforts to ensure that she felt taken care of and provided for on a material level. Of course, I failed miserably in doing the same for her emotionally. But how could I not have? I was always running, petrified of being discovered, and so I never devoted any time to sitting still and providing needs that required me to be honest. I was never available to understand, never mind provide for, her deeper heartfelt and emotional needs. I was never present. And I hated myself for that.

I attempted to be the best father my children could imagine. Fully engaged in family outings, playtime activities, shopping, helping with homework, giving baths, changing diapers, sharing mealtimes together, spending time on the floor in the playroom, and reading bedtime stories. I gladly participated in nurturing, protecting, and providing for private Jewish day school education for our six children born within eight years. And yet, I never knew how to be a strong role model for them. How could I? I was a woman disguised as their father.

While my undying, unconditional love for my children was true and real, I could not generate an authentic fatherly persona. As their father, I felt I was failing them. The role I felt most suited for was already taken. I did not know how to truly nurture them, to protect them, and to teach them as a man, so I mimicked the other Orthodox Chassidic men with whom I intermingled. I trained myself to mimic their actions, like a circus animal. Others may have seen me as a father who met and often exceeded his parental responsibilities, but I saw nothing but disgust and impotence when I looked in the mirror.

As a son to my parents, I was expected to assume increasing leadership of the family business. I was not only to maintain the company, but to bring it to an even greater level of success. A business that I had no desire to be a part of. A business that drained me by the mere thought of having to physically be in its environs. A business completely irrelevant to my true passion of teaching Torah. As with any business, it was driven by the entrepreneurial motive to yield financial gains. It idealized the "mom-and-pop" profit-driven enterprise, the success of the post-WWII middle class.

My father's company was an honest business, built by a hardworking man with sound values, based on treating everyone honestly and ethically. But I was not created to be a businessperson. I was especially unsuited to run a plumbing supply business that catered to and was supported by an all-male, blue-collar customer base. Although I never had trouble being with or communicating with the customers themselves, this work was emotionally draining for me because it lacked any deep sense of intellectual or spiritual fulfillment. I was so desperate to please my father and to make him proud that once again I throttled into autopilot gear and went through the motions, like a young boy seeking an affectionate pat on the head. But the motions were just that—lacking spirit, lacking soul, lacking passion, and clearly lacking health.

And then there was my role in the community of Lubavitchers. Once again, I found myself performing as a well-trained circus animal. I would drive the 120 miles round-trip to and from Brooklyn to buy kosher products certified by rabbis applying the highest standards of supervision. I brought my wife and children back and forth to Crown Heights every week so they could nurture connections with like-minded Jewish people. Staying with friends for Shabbat and holidays became standard. It seemed like I was always driving from point A to point B, and then back again. But I was getting nowhere.

At times I would attend the farbrengens, Yiddish for the very well-attended public gatherings when the Lubavitcher Rebbe would speak to and teach his thousands of followers and admirers. How could I not attend? Even though I did not understand the language that the Rebbe spoke, and even though each time I entered the huge assembly hall I once again was cruelly thrust into this all-male locker room that made me feel dirty and dishonest, I came. Even though I knew I belonged up above in the women's section, I did what any typical Lubavitch man longed to do. With black hat snugly perched on my head, I played my part in the charade. More than once, an innocent, naïve individual would remind me how blessed we were to be where we were, exclaiming that Crown Heights was even holier than the Holy Land itself. This to me was the ultimate untruth, for more than anything I longed to be back in Israel.

After a long week of pretending to be what I was not in my father's business, these trips drained what little energy I had left. In a way, they were all the same. I dreaded them. That is, I dreaded them when I allowed myself to feel the excruciating pain of the black hole that I felt myself being sucked deeper and deeper into. When I did not allow myself access to these raw emotions, I simply went through the motions in a lifeless manner. It is hard to say which was worse.

My life was a lie that extended from dawn to dusk. At times I would ask myself if I was condemned to living in this barren, frigid wilderness my entire life. Most of the time I sadly resigned myself to answering "yes."

Chapter 17

IT'S MY TURN NOW

On my thirty-third birthday, July 3, 1984, I gave myself a special gift: my one-year notice to my father that I was leaving his business, selling my home and car, and moving my family back to Israel. At least as troublesome as my own internal gender identity disorder was my struggle to survive in the Diaspora. The relentless stress of living outside Israel and inside a body that was not my own had taken its toll on me. At thirty-three I felt closer to ninety-three—old, aged without grace, and lifeless.

This state of being was suffocating whatever life I was still desperately holding on to. I felt I was trapped in a space that was shrinking. It was only a matter of time before I would no longer be able to move or even breathe. I was clinging to life as I lay in a coffin whose lid was closing in on me. I needed air. I yearned for air. I longed to live in the one place on earth where I felt that simply breathing would keep me somewhat alive. Being at home, inhaling and exhaling the air in Israel, would be lifesaving, even with the severe inner struggle I experienced around my gender. I felt compelled to return to my home, to Israel, and this time to Jerusalem. Any chance I ever had of living an authentic life, I convinced myself, could occur only there. That was as real as I could have been with myself at that moment.

On this day, I felt hope for the first time since leaving Israel in July 1979. I felt encouragement. I felt I would somehow have a chance, in ways still unknown to me, to live a normal life. If at least my family and I lived where my Zionist ideals urged me to be, I might change the course of my torturous journey.

In fact, our return to Israel did exactly that, and in ways I could never have imagined.

I told my parents, "One year from today, on July 3, 1985, I am returning home to Jerusalem. It's my turn now."

PART THREE

IT ALL COMES TUMBLING DOWN
1985–1992

Chapter 18

IT WILL TAKE A MIRACLE

There was no job awaiting me. I had nothing more than a two-bedroom apartment to live in temporarily, and no definite plans other than to arrive and somehow move my entourage of a family to the Old City of Jerusalem. So, off we went! Unlike Lot's wife in the biblical account of leaving Sodom, I made sure not to turn around and look back. As far as I was concerned, if I never returned to that part of the world again I would be most grateful. On July 3, 1979, my twenty-eighth birthday, I left Tzfat, Israel. On July 3, 1985, my thirty-fourth birthday, I returned home to Israel, this time to the Old City of Jerusalem, where my journey had begun fourteen years earlier.

I had no idea how I was going to pull this off, from many perspectives. Jewish tradition strongly believes in miracles, as evidenced throughout the Bible and in rabbinic literature. At times a miracle clearly defies the laws of nature. Other times they convince the believer that Divine intervention has been revealed to him or her. However, as strongly as Jewish communities teach the younger generation to believe in miracles, we are also warned not to depend on them.

I conveniently disregarded this second teaching and completely depended on experiencing not one but several miracles upon my return home. I became an expert in convincing my wife as well that everything would work out, having no idea how this would come to be.

I also lived with the false illusion that by moving almost 6,000 miles away, I would leave my problems behind me. My demons were not welcome in Jerusalem. I was genuinely desperate, and desperately committed to living a good life, a normal life, the religious Zionist dream, and to honoring my soul. Simply put, my inner demons that had plagued me for the first thirty-four years of my life played no role in my dream world. I reasoned, or rather fantasized, that having gone to this extent, moving my family around the world to follow His word, surely God would do His part and slay the dragons on my behalf.

But I had seriously underestimated the power of my inner demons, and their evil intent to destroy me. My life was a tragedy waiting to happen.

I shipped an entire container's worth of material possessions—furniture, clothing, kitchenware, linens and bedding, books, knickknacks, toys and games, and more toys and more games and more clothing. Of course, I made sure not to ship my inner turmoil. I left that in Patchogue, where it was born and where I wanted it to die so I could bury it. It would not and could not be shipped. I ordered the decree that it remain in the Diaspora, sentenced to death by my own inner Supreme Court.

I hired a van to transport us—my wife and me and our six children aged nine years to nine months—the fifty miles to JFK Airport for our El Al flight to Israel. We had close to twenty pieces of luggage to be checked at the airport, not one of which contained my inner strife. The excruciating, chronic pain of my gender identity disorder had extended to every crevice of my being. But I decided that there was no place for it on this return flight to Israel. I convinced myself I was off to a new start.

When a person moves, Jewish people offer the blessing "Change the place, change the luck." If anyone desperately clung to these well-meaning words, it was me. God was giving me a second chance to return home, and this time I was not going to sabotage it. Entertaining my inner demons threatened this longed-for opportunity, so I dismissed them. As if I had waved a magic wand over my inner being, I pushed them down so deep that for a short time they gave me respite. I boarded the plane with my family feeling clean, eager, and grateful.

For a fleeting moment, I knew this was a charade, a false illusion. For a split second, I knew I was lying to myself. But it was time to settle the kids and buckle our seat belts in preparation for takeoff. Those feelings remained lodged in the deep recesses of my consciousness, but I refused to acknowledge them.

In less than twenty-four hours, I convinced myself that all bridges behind me had been burnt to the ground, and as soon as possible I returned to the Western Wall, once again, to thank God for going along with my plan. In less than a week, we were marginally settled in our new little temporary home, I started teaching, and we began the process of integrating into religious Israeli society.

And while I was warned never to depend on a miracle, in fact I did, and in fact that is exactly what it took for this monumental move to occur. At that point, in July 1985, I never could have imagined or prepared myself for how this miracle would impact my journey and my future. All I could do at that point was to falsely believe I had actually rid myself of the evil forces that had handicapped me from living a healthy life for thirty-four years.

Chapter 19

MY SUCCESS WAS MY FAILURE

My deception accelerated into fifth gear. As if the past six years had existed only in my nightmares, in no time I fell back into my former life. It almost seemed too easy. Returning to my passion, I assumed a leadership position in Jewish education in the rebuilt Jewish Quarter. I both created content and taught for several highly reputable institutions, including the Chabad House of the Old City. The programming focused on the Anglo, English-speaking population, both those who had moved to Israel and those students and tourists who were visiting.

My role as a Jewish educator extended beyond the classroom to my home. The clearly drawn boundary between my public work life and private family and social life began to blur. It blurred to such an extent that the line all but disappeared as it faded into the background. My home and family were on display for all to see. Teaching led to Sabbath and holiday meal hosting with upwards of twenty-five people in our home at one time. Without any intention, my family and I lived in the spotlight. We somehow gained the reputation of being the perfect, ideal, happy success story of a growing religious Zionist and Chassidic family. The fact that neither my wife nor I came from a religiously observant family, nor Israel, enhanced the beauty of this perfect picture. People would sit in my classes or at my dinner table and seek a spiritual experience that would be their own personal epiphany. And I did not want to disappoint them. My outward rise to fame, my external success beyond anyone's imagination, translated into my own sense of tremendous inner failure. I knew this was wrong.

Outwardly, I only wanted to do right by God, by me, by my family, and by my community. Inwardly, I felt like a fraud. As I desperately attempted to survive this masquerade, the words that came out of my mouth were wonderful, inspirational, and filled with passion. These were words taught by the Jewish sages over thousands and thousands of years throughout Jewish history.

Throughout this time in my life, my most important student was myself. I convinced myself that if I taught with enough passion, enough preparation, enough commitment to being a stellar educator, host, and family "man," just maybe I would have a chance of a normal life. So many people whom I met during those years acknowledged that I never pressured them to "become religious" as so many other educators did. But what they did not know was that the only student whom I became obsessed with trying to convince, to pressure, to even manipulate, was myself. I had no energy to even try those disrespectful tactics on anyone else. Finding my own redemption and even salvation consumed me.

Soon years had passed like this, in a blur. And finally those demons, those evil spirits, those powers within me who sought to tear down my façade, began to wake up with a vengeance. Of course, they followed me to Israel, and even pursued me. Of course, they boarded the plane with me. Like a glass of water spilling on a counter, they found their way into every single crevice of my life. They made their presence known in the synagogue, at the Western Wall, in the middle of a lecture to 200 eager students, at the Shabbat table, when playing with my children, during fund-raising lectures and classes abroad, when going on family outings to the beach and on nature hikes. They even managed to viciously seep into the most frightening place in my life—my consciousness.

I could no longer go on a simple errand to buy a dozen eggs by myself. I could no longer simply walk down the street in downtown Jerusalem. I could no longer lay my head down on the pillow at night and drift off to a peaceful night's sleep. I went to bed with knots in my stomach, and I woke up short of breath.

On Friday nights as I would leave the Western Wall, I slowly, very slowly, made my way home. People thought I was immersed in the restful Sabbath energy. Nothing could have been further from the truth. As I approached my home, with my children in tow, and a crowd of all kinds of people from all over the world following me, anticipating their version of the perfect Jewish spiritual experience, all I could feel were those pressing knots in my stomach. I simply, completely dreaded the hours during which my acting ability, like the image I portrayed, had to be perfect.

I felt that increasingly after each class, lecture, group meal, holiday, or fund-raising trip abroad, another part of my soul was amputated, leaving me increasingly numb. At a certain point, I just stopped feeling. My personal fifth gear was survival mode, an almost primal, primitive experience. I knew it was only a matter of time before this huge skyscraper of a life that I had built, a life that soared high into the clouds, would tumble down. How could it not? It lacked a foundation. Nothing but desperation and fear held it together.

I began to dread everything I did. How could this be happening? I would constantly ask myself. The sense of fraud compounded daily. I was no longer able to appreciate whatever good I did on behalf of others. My wife, my children, my students, my neighbors, my colleagues, and my community were deceived by my very life. And the more I did, the more I deceived them. I was swept up by this tornado as my life began to spin out of control. All I could feel, when I allowed myself to feel, was failure and disgust.

This state of affairs encountered yet another unforeseen obstacle of gigantic proportions. The threat of war was looming in the background. As my domestic life began to fall apart, so did the world around me. The Gulf War crisis began when I was in weekly therapy, attempting to piece together whatever I could to keep my family from completely falling apart. In January 1991, when Saddam Hussein fired the first Scud missile at Israel, I needed to manage my own internal crisis. It was as if the missiles were a metaphor for what was happening to my internal life. No gas mask, no safe room, and no amount of preparation could have protected me from this onslaught seeking to destroy me, and by extension, my family.

And of course, I was my own personal Saddam Hussein. I became my own inner personal Scud missile. I felt the deception of my life begin to crumble. My own commitment to leading a life of Torah could no longer battle the horrific war raging within me. My own gender identity disorder refused to be repressed any longer, and now relentlessly attacked me.

And the war raged on. As soon as the first missile was fired, all programming in the Jewish Quarter came to a screeching halt as most of the Anglo students and tourists rushed to Ben Gurion Airport before it closed down. I lost my livelihood and one of my last remaining sources of pleasure and fulfillment—my career.

For several months leading up to this point in time, I received professional intervention from a psychiatrist. I could not move further along my journey alone. I needed help. Week after week, Dr. Quinn would begin each session with the same question. He would ask, "How are you feeling?" I would then answer his question, or so I thought. This would be the lead-in to that day's topic.

One week, when Dr. Quinn asked me how I was feeling, I answered, "I am petrified. I am so scared right now." To my utter disbelief, he smiled at me. I asked him how he could smile at such a statement. I knew my life was falling apart. I knew my marriage of almost eighteen years was soon to be over. I knew my family would be torn apart. I was so scared, and my psychiatrist was smiling!

He told me that for the first time under his care, I had actually answered his question. I had told him how I felt rather than what I was thinking, which had been my modus operandi for the past several months. He then said, "Now we can begin your therapy."

After that pivotal and draining therapy session, all I could do was go directly to the Western Wall and do something I had not done in my entire life. I buried my face into the cold, wet stones in the Jerusalem winter, now under attack, and I cried. I wept uncontrollably. I wept for the almost forty years I'd spent suffering a miserable, torturous life. I wept for the hurt I knew I would cause those I loved the most, my family. I wept and wept and wept. The lie was over.

My success was truly my failure. And yet, it was the very beginning of my real success, my own redemption, my own salvation from my inner demons. But on that wet, cold, lonely day, immersed as I was in such fear and pain, I could not entertain such truth.

Chapter 20

AND THE MAN FOUND YOSEF

In the course of a lifetime, there are people who can change our lives in an instant. Those people create experiences for us that, however brief, can profoundly impact, or even define, the rest of our lives.

This very scenario happened to the biblical character Yosef (Joseph)—and to me as well.

As recounted in the Bible, Yaakov (Jacob) sends his son Yosef to find his brothers, who are away seeking new pastures to tend the family flock. Yaakov wants Yosef to check if they and the flock are well. He is told to return with his report, but Yosef cannot find them, feels somewhat lost, and wanders:

A man discovered him, and behold!—he was blundering in the field; the man asked him, saying, "What do you seek?" And he said, "My brothers do I seek; tell me, please, where they are pasturing." The man said, "They have journeyed on from here, for I heard them saying, 'Let us go to Dothan.'" So, Yosef went after his brothers and found them at Dothan. (Genesis 37:15–17)

This encounter, at first glance, seems to be nothing extraordinary. And yet, it defined the rest of Jewish history. It would have been easy and even within reason for Yosef to have turned around and returned home. He surely could have explained to his father that he simply could not find his brothers. Instead, out of a deep sense of loyalty to his father, he felt compelled to persistently search for them. While searching, not knowing where to go, a "man" discovers him.

We are never told who this "man" is. We are never told if he ever reappears in Yosef's life. What the Bible does tell us is that after this encounter, Yosef did find his brothers, who abducted him and sold him into slavery. He was brought into Egypt, and after a series of strange events he ascended from being a prisoner to becoming the viceroy and second-in-command to Pharaoh. A famine then occurred in Israel, Yaakov sent his remaining sons to Egypt to purchase food, and Yaakov, once again through a series of unpredictable events, was reunited with his cherished son for whom he had been in mourning for many years. Yaakov moved his family of seventy to live near Yosef, and his family was spared starving to death from the famine in Israel. This small tribal family of seventy grew into a nation of millions, was enslaved by the Egyptians, was redeemed and freed 210 years later, left Egypt, traveled through the wilderness for forty years, and eventually settled in the Land of Israel.

The rabbinical commentaries teach that the "man" who initiated this complex chain of events was the angel Gavriel (Gabriel). God sent Gavriel to help guide Yosef to this pivotal moment that in turn defined the rest of Jewish history.

In the years 1985–1991, I wandered like Yosef. I too felt compelled to persistently search. Unlike Yosef, though, I had no idea what I was searching for. What was clear to me was that I was living another person's life. It was a good life, a wonderful life, a life based in spiritualty and in time-honored, God-given ethics and values. I lived a life that dated back to the Yosef story itself. But it wasn't my life. It belonged to the image of the person I projected to all those around me. But it wasn't the authentic me. This person was a good person, but it was not me, living my truth.

The definition of my own life and how I wanted it to look evaded me. I had no idea. I didn't even know what it was I was supposed to do, where to go, or what to say to whom. What I did know was that I was lost. Similar to Yosef, I was "blundering in the field."

And then I met my own angel. There was a "man" who discovered me, and in a brief encounter lasting no longer than a few minutes, he profoundly and clearly changed the rest of my life.

Not too long before the Gulf War broke out in January 1991, on a Friday night, I experienced an extraordinarily painful walk back home from the Western Wall. Every Friday night brought with it dread and pain, but this night in particular brought with it a higher dose. As I walked up the hill to my home, with a group of guests loyally following me, I told HaShem, "NO!" I screamed out to HaShem, quietly, to please do something so this would not continue. I had nothing left within me to continue this charade, wearing a mask and hiding the real me from the world.

I managed to say my lines and go through the actions on cue as I did every Friday night, but I knew it was without soul. Something felt wrong. It was more contrived than ever. It was so painful. It hurt. I kept telling myself that this would pass—it always did.

Finally, it was time for everyone to leave. Usually as the guests would leave, they would shower my wife and me with endless expressions of gratitude and praise. Each expression was like a knife turning in my heart. This was always the worst part of the evening for me.

Tonight was very different, though. The guests were polite and expressed their appreciation for our hospitality. However, the usual outpouring of praise did not accompany their good-byes.

One man in particular, "the" man, asked me in a low voice if he could speak to me alone for a minute. I told him of course, but dreaded what I thought he would say to me. I expected an extra dose of praise. Instead, he said, "Please understand that what I am going to say to you comes from a place of concern for your well-being. That was an amazing act you just performed for all of us over the past several hours. You are in such pain, and I can see it. Please take care of yourself." He then left. I did not know his name, nor did I ever see him again. Our only private interchange, as with Yosef and "the man," lasted a minute at most.

I told my wife what had happened, and we never had any guests over again. That night I slept like a baby. That night I thanked HaShem for sending me the angel Gavriel to save me from myself, to save my life.

Chapter 21

LIFE WILL NEVER BE THE SAME

From January to March 1991, I endured immense spiritual, emotional, and mental upheaval. Heartbreaking and profoundly sad does not begin to describe the experience of anticipating the dissolution of my marriage and family. Nothing before or since has been as painful to me. I could not have imagined an opportune time to dismantle my family, but had such a time existed, it surely was not in the winter of 1991 in Israel.

Any attempt I made to minimize the pain and trauma for everyone was countered by the Gulf War. In the middle of such a horrific domestic catastrophe hitting my nuclear family, sirens would ring at unpredictable times of the day and night. Uncertainty, instability, and fear of the unknown immediate future gripped us all. On those nights, we woke up our children, who were already frightened and bordering on being in shock, and we moved as quickly as possible to the safe room, making sure everyone had a gas mask, never knowing if the next missile would have a chemical warhead attached to it. The war further embittered an already bitter experience.

As if the process of finally facing my demons and filing for divorce wasn't enough, I had to make sure that I took my gas mask with me when I went to meetings with my lawyer and my rabbi. Clutching the device that would save my physical life in the event of an attack, I managed to go through the painful steps I needed to take in order to save myself spiritually and emotionally.

Instead of devoting my life to being in relationship with God and seeking Divine guidance, I had sought to control all the minutiae of every waking second of my life. I lived in constant fear that if I did not exert complete control over my life, it would fall apart. But this is exactly what happened. My life as I came to know it came tumbling down. I felt the ground upon which I established myself completely fall out from under me. I was pulled underground, falling down a dark, bottomless hole with no end in sight, just bracing myself for the moment of inevitable impact.

I had nothing to lean on, no one to depend on, no one to cry out to. Not for a second did it occur to me at that time to cry out to God for help.

Not only did I break down, I took my whole family down with me. Any guilt I already had paled in comparison to realizing what pain I caused those closest to me. It was a true miracle, literally, that I did not simply collapse into a paralyzing mental coma.

And then, the fateful day of my divorce arrived. In Israel, the Rabbinate oversees all marriages and divorces. When the religious court communicates to a husband and wife that they are expected to present themselves on a designated date to dissolve their marriage, one is expected to obey. It had not occurred to me to suggest to my rabbi that we wait until the international crisis ended before dissolving the domestic one. But on the very morning we were scheduled to go to the Beit Din, the religious court, in March 1991, Iraq officially announced that it would cease firing missiles at Israel.

For the first time since early January, I left my home without carrying my gas mask. A big, heavy weight had literally been compassionately lifted from my shoulders. I felt lighter. I felt grateful. I even sensed a small ray of optimism. These feelings were mixed with dread, fear, nervousness—and guilt, the likes of which I would not have wished on anyone, except perhaps the evil Saddam Hussein.

I entered the court married and left single and divorced. Completely heartbroken and immersed in sadness, I still felt relieved. Perhaps for the first time in my life, I had actually done something completely honest. I deceived no one. My decision to go through with this step became a source of honor and integrity for me. I did what any decent, honest human being would have done in the same position. For finally doing something, even something as radical and drastic as dissolving a marriage and family, I was rewarded with a clear conscience for the first time in my life.

If only it hadn't been necessary to hurt so many people. Why had it taken a painful divorce to begin to live in authenticity? Clearly, I was in no position to reconcile this dilemma as I left the courtroom. Still, I knew life would never be the same, and I breathed freely with that knowledge.

On that day, I felt unstable, insecure, overwhelmed with confusion, and acutely guilty. I felt like a complete failure as a human being, and a source of disappointment to every single person who knew me. But I also felt relief for the first time in my life. Oddly, I felt no fear. Gratefully, I felt clean.

Yes, life would never be the same. At last .

Chapter 22

SAYING GOOD-BYE

After twenty years of being in a relationship and building a family with my wife, I said good-bye to my marriage. After six years of living in Jerusalem, it was coming time to leave that place as well.

Since Saddam Hussein was no longer firing missiles at Israel, tourists and students started returning to the Jewish Quarter to participate in various Jewish learning programs. Not for a moment did I consider leaving my teaching position. However, no one from the school contacted me to let me know that programming was resuming. Intuitively, I sensed the red flag looming, and yet, I could not have guessed how "red."

After seeing posters throughout the Jewish Quarter advertising the resumption of various classes and lectures, I went to the school's administration office. I needed to know what and when I would be teaching again. From the moment

I walked into the office, I sensed danger. It was only too clear that people I'd known and worked closely with for years chose to ignore me. I barely succeeded in eliciting a few hellos. Finally, I spoke up and asked to speak with the person responsible for coordinating my schedule. Without even looking at me, rather almost looking away from me, he curtly and coldly said I was not welcome back to teach. I was stunned! He mustered up the excuse that since I was now divorced, I was no longer a proper role model for the students. With that, he walked away and I was in no uncertain terms told to leave.

I walked out in shock. What would I do now? Where would I work? I had a family to support. I was considered to be one of their most stellar educators, and now I was tossed out into the street because I was no longer "a proper role model." I knew that this pitiful excuse was masking something larger. It would not be long before I found out what that was.

During the months leading up to the divorce, both in therapy and in meetings with my rabbi, I did not disclose the true reason why I sought the separation. In 1991, with no access to information beyond my limited environment, I believed I was the only person on the planet suffering from having been born female but held hostage in a male body. Terms such as gender identity disorder, gender dysphoria, transgender, and transition remained alien to me at the time. I had no idea that thousands of other individuals throughout the world suffered as I did.

How could I tell the truth to my wife? To my therapist? To my rabbi? I convinced myself that through a collaborative effort they would report me to the proper authorities, who would commit me to a psychiatric hospital for treatment. Therefore, I told everyone that I was gay. I left one lie behind only to enter another. I knew without a doubt that I was a straight heterosexual female, but nothing in my reality allowed me to be that honest. So, I lied. Of course, I assumed this information would be kept strictly confidential. I assumed wrong.

Very soon after learning that I was not welcome back at the very yeshiva that had touted me as one of their best educators, I received a peculiar phone call. One of the major Orthodox rabbinical leaders in Jerusalem personally called me and requested that I come to his office. He needed to speak with me about an urgent matter. Alarms, bells, and whistles went off in my mind. He seldom called anyone himself but rather delegated this task to his personal secretary. The rabbi made it clear that there was no room for me to negotiate any other day or time to meet. He even emphasized that I was not to be late. The phone call was short, cold, and ominous.

I arrived, with trepidation, to his home. He was considered to be one of the leading rabbinical authorities in Jerusalem, and people would wait in line for hours to seek his advice and counsel. When I arrived, there were no lines. As with the phone call, he himself answered the door rather than his secretary. He barely looked at me and ushered me into his office.

In very clear English, so as not to be misunderstood, he told me the following: "Do not sit down, as I will make this quick. It has come to my attention that you have been teaching Torah to young men in the Jewish Quarter for the past several years. It has also come to my attention that you are guilty of committing the disgusting, perverted sin of lying with a man like a woman. As of now you are prohibited from ever teaching men in Jerusalem again. And if you choose to continue teaching men in Jerusalem, your children will be publicly humiliated."

I felt my body shake, and my eyes began to tear up. All I could muster up as a meek reply was "Are you threatening me?"

He replied, "Absolutely. If you have any love for your children, which is highly questionable, take me very seriously."

In tears, I asked him, "What am I supposed to do? I need to support my family."

He replied, "Go teach women in Tzfat. Now leave my office. I can't even look at you anymore. You are despicable and disgusting."

I walked out stunned, and I don't even recall how I made it home. I walked in the door, stood in the kitchen, and removed my kippah—the traditional head covering worn by Jewish males. I never put it back on, except at a few family celebrations. I felt so violated, so betrayed, and for the first time I could recall I was livid with the rabbis! The very establishment for whom I had constantly tried to prove myself as being worthy, as being good, as being right, the people on whom I depended to teach me how to live a life of truth and how to be kind and compassionate, had betrayed me. I promised myself right then and there that I would never empower anyone again to legitimize my Judaism, nor to define my relationship with God.

Of course, deep down, I was angriest with myself. I betrayed myself, I violated myself, I trespassed my own boundaries of integrity by not living a life of authenticity. I worshiped the foreign idol of acceptance due to my fear and self-delusion, and I paid a dear price for this. I never worshipped God. I never engaged in a real relationship with God. I never truly dedicated my life to God, but rather to others. This was modern idol worship, for which I was guilty.

In Jewish tradition, when the same type of event happens three times, it is considered to be a sign of confirmation and affirmation. After being rejected at my school and by a major rabbi in Jerusalem, I passed by two women who knew me as a community member and educator. Out of their sight, I overheard one say to the other, "And did you hear what happened to those poor Smith children? Their parents so selfishly divorced and split up the family. What were they thinking? Clearly only of themselves and not of their children."

This was too much for me to bear. I knew it was time to leave. It was time to leave both the Jewish Quarter in the Old City and Orthodox Judaism. From 1971 to 1991, I was on a trajectory leading to what I hoped would be a normal and good life. Instead, I was heading straight toward disaster. My dream to live a religious, Jewish, spiritually based life in Israel withered away. I tried so hard to live someone else's life, but it was doomed to fail from the onset.

Before I left the Old City, I visited a special woman who shared with me a secret about myself from which I would come to draw incredible strength. I had made an appointment with an observant Jewish astrological therapist. I had tried other forms of therapy, so why not give this one a chance? She asked for the exact date, time, and place of my birth, and used that to create a "birth chart." More involved than a traditional horoscope, a birth chart diagrams the exact placement of all the planets, the sun, and the moon at the moment of one's birth. This therapist claimed that she could use the chart to analyze my personality and the trajectories of my life.

I sat down at her table and saw the huge chart she had created for me, a detailed map of the solar system. The therapist explained to me that, based on the positioning of the various planets, the stars, and the moon at my birth, she could see certain traits of mine that I might or might not be aware of. From her understanding of what she saw on the chart, she was going to describe a few traits that she felt were essential for me to acknowledge and act upon if I hoped to live a life of well-being and inner peace. At this point, I neither believed her nor rejected her. After all, who was I to even have an opinion?

She proceeded to tell me some things about myself that I already knew, and a few that were new but not surprising. And then it happened. She told me something about myself that I had carefully safeguarded from every single human being I had ever encountered. This was my best-kept secret, hidden far away in the deepest recesses within my psyche.

She said that, based on the positioning of Mars and the moon, and maybe a few other planets, and which ones were ascending and which descending, I had "extremely excessive female energy," to the point that my female energy was as far to the extreme as possible. Of course, I did not understand how she arrived at this conclusion by looking at my birth chart, but she clearly was the first person in my life who discovered my secret. And this I did understand!

She spoke with no judgment, and she offered no suggestion as to what to do about this knowledge or what this meant. All she said was that until I honored and expressed this, I would not achieve a life of inner peace and health.

I had been excommunicated by my own community, by the very people from whom I sought acceptance and respect. I had been distanced from my children, and I knew that soon I would remove myself from both my physical and my spiritual home in Jerusalem. But I also knew that once and for all, my gender identity could no longer be denied or ignored. It was making its way to the surface at long last.

Chapter 23

NO PLACE FOR ME

On July 3, 1991, for the first time in my life, I woke up on my birthday alone. It was my fortieth birthday, and I was all alone. No family, no wife, no close friends. This was not supposed to be my life script. This was not the part I wanted to play.

I felt alone and lonely, yes. But the good news was: I was feeling! I experienced my own feelings and not someone else's. I felt vulnerable, naked, and defenseless. I felt real! I felt, in the modest little studio I'd rented in Tel Aviv, as the salty Mediterranean breeze gently brushed my face, that I was in fact waking up to myself for the first time, to my life, with all its uncertainties and questions and pain.

I also woke up to guilt. I imagined all my children with their mother, waking up on my fortieth birthday to their own uncertainty, no less naked and vulnerable than me. I sighed.

Perhaps most importantly, what I realized on my fortieth birthday was that life would not always be black or white, that not every question needed a yes-or-no answer. Life was all about living in the gray, dwelling in the space of ambiguity. Allowing myself to embrace this truth for the very first time in my life was the birthday gift I generously and compassionately gave to myself.

The first thing I had to do after I left Jerusalem and moved to Tel Aviv was to officially come out to myself, expelling my demons once and for all in my own ritual act of exorcism. I had read articles about the transformative experience of coming out to oneself—feeling relief and joy at uttering the words "I am gay" aloud while looking into a mirror.

So, now it was my turn. Since the divorce I'd been living in a blur, encountering one emotionally charged moment after another. For much of the past few months, I had been reacting to other people's decisions. Now I felt compelled to reclaim a sliver of my own capacity to be proactive and do something for my own well-being.

I walked into the bathroom and stared at myself in the mirror. I hesitated for several minutes, although it seemed like hours. I felt like a taut rubber band, stretched to my breaking point. I was hesitant but committed, confused but resolved, limited but expansive.

The only way to avoid being torn apart any further by these forces was to come clean and say it. So, I did. I looked deeply into my own eyes and said, "I am gay. I am gay. I am gay."

I cried and cried, but I did not feel the lightness I had anticipated, nor the sense of relief I expected. The heavy burden I had carried all my life was not lifted from me. In fact, I felt terrible, dirty, and ashamed. My burden had only grown heavier.

I looked into the mirror even harder and longer, and I thought to myself, "I am not gay. I am a woman. I am a heterosexual woman. I am female. I am not a gay man." Those words, however, I could not yet utter aloud. I traded in one lie for another. Instead of pretending to be a straight man, I now pretended to be a gay man.

If only I had known that there were thousands of fellow human beings throughout the world suffering as me. If only I had had the language to express who I really was, maybe then I could have come out of the closet completely, rather than finding a new closet in which to hide. To be a salmon swimming upstream (even in the company of other salmon) was difficult enough, especially for someone who had lived for forty years swimming downstream with the multitudes. However, to be the only salmon? Clearly, I was not ready for that.

Just as I had lied to both the Orthodox and non-Orthodox worlds in Jerusalem, I now began my new masquerade as a gay man in Tel Aviv. But this time I knew with resounding clarity that this lie would be short lived. I knew now that these sorts of lies were not sustainable, especially since they erode one's sense of self-respect, self-esteem, and integrity. I would not let this happen again. I just needed time to figure out what to do and how to do it, time to adjust to being divorced, to living apart from my children, and to being without a support system. I needed to strategize. So, for the meantime at least, I honored the one part of me that was completely true—my natural attraction as a woman to men.

* * *

Soon after my birthday, I found a job paying minimal wages at a travel company, organizing group tours for

European tourists. A few months earlier, I had been teaching spiritually hungry young men and women how to navigate and experience their spiritual journeys. Now I was arranging for adult European tourists to navigate and experience their physical journey to Israel. Such a stark contrast. At the very least, I knew my work would influence the souls of my clients, if only indirectly. That provided some respite.

My social life was just as minimally satisfying. Unsuccessfully, I attempted to integrate or at least connect with the gay Israeli community in Tel Aviv. The men I met were significantly younger than me, both biologically and in life experience. Most had been in the army, which further distanced me from them. Excluding the occasional Anglo immigrant, they spoke very little English, and my Hebrew skills did not allow me to fully participate in their discussions.

They were friendly to me, and kind. But I was always a guest and never regarded as "one of them." I didn't blame them. After all, how could I truly be a part of their world? Aside from all the obvious differences, I was a woman attempting to integrate into an all-male environment. Not unlike the segregated culture of ultra-Orthodox Jerusalem, the gay community of Tel Aviv seldom engaged with women at all. In fact, they seemed committed to avoiding being in the company of women as much as possible.

So, once again I didn't fit in. And this time I had no children to come home to, no women entering my home to chat with. I looked forward to going to work if for no other reason than it was a predominantly female office where I felt very comfortable.

Each Friday, the office would close early, as was the practice of most businesses in Israel. Observant or not, it was Erev Shabbat, the afternoon preceding the Sabbath. Most stores would be closed on Shabbat, even in Tel Aviv, where bars, clubs, and restaurants would remain open. Leaving work early gave Israelis time to shop for food and other necessities for Shabbat.

Instead of anticipating dozens of assorted people following me home from the Western Wall on a Friday night, I now spent most Shabbat evenings alone. No fancy dinners. No singing. No group get-togethers. No children singing and playing and telling everyone what they had learned at school during the week. Also, I no longer felt knots in my stomach. But it was lonely, very lonely. Each Shabbat night I would walk along the beach and reflect on how much I loved Shabbat, and how my journey had led me to a place where I had come to dread it. Now, I missed it terribly. Instead of being with friends or family, I would go to the bars. I would go to the dance clubs. I would go out to eat from time to time with some of my newly made acquaintances. Once again, I began living someone else's life. The real me faded away.

By February, the sheer loneliness and lack of purpose in my life began to push me, mentally and emotionally, out of Israel. I dreaded leaving my children, who would visit each week. Their visits were what I lived for. Their visits made me feel alive, even if they were only for one afternoon and night a week. And even more importantly, my children needed me to continue providing some kind of presence in their lives. Perhaps the strongest instinctive need of a parent, especially one who felt and continues to feel more maternal than paternal, is to protect one's children and safeguard their well-being. I already knew I had painfully failed my children in this most important area of child rearing. But at least they were able to be with me once a week, and for them this was essential.

I hated myself for not giving my children what they needed from me, but I knew I had to go. I was feeling pushed out.

After twenty years, it was time to finally realize that there was no place for me in Israel. That thought was perhaps the darkest cloud I ever had to face in my life. There is no place like home, and yet, there was no place for me to be at home.

In Leviticus we read:

Defile not ye yourselves in any of these things; for in all these the nations are defiled, which I cast out from before you. And the land was defiled, therefore I did visit the iniquity thereof upon it, and the land vomited out her inhabitants…that the land vomit not you out also, when ye defile it, as it vomited out the nation that was before you. (18:24, 25, 28)

At this moment of my life, on the way to the airport, with my head down, every dream I ever had, except one, evaporated and disappeared into thin air. I felt as though I were being ejected, vomited out of the Land of Israel. One dream still remained with me and accompanied me to the airport—the dream to live a life of truth and to be honest with myself and with everyone around me.

PART FOUR

PLUNGING INTO DARKNESS AND DESPAIR
1992–2001

Chapter 24

BARELY HOLDING ON

Feeling orphaned and displaced in the winter of 1992, I went to the only spot on the planet that still felt familiar—Manhattan. I felt that I had betrayed God, and even worse, that God had betrayed me. I was angry and hurt. In Israel I traded one lie for another and packed this new lie in my suitcase en route to New York. Instead of living as a heterosexual Jewish, Orthodox, married-with-children male, I began living as a gay, nonobservant single, effeminate male. I felt as disconnected from myself and from the gay men I attempted to be in community with as I did from myself and from the Orthodox men by whom I had been surrounded for the past twenty years. Each day during this period, and for the following nine years, I felt alone, lonely, and distant from both my real self and the world at large. Denying myself a life dedicated to honoring my own individual truth exacted a price higher than I could ever have imagined. My very humanity was being chipped away day by day, little by little.

Unlike my previous lie, this new perversion of the truth brought with it a degree of relief. Living alone spared me the daily repetitive anguish of lying to the people I loved the most. I was an imposter by day, but by night I had no one to fool anymore, not even myself.

However, the acute guilt I felt for the pain I caused my family followed me back to New York. There it evolved into a chronic, gnawing state of being. A layer of complexity embittered my guilt even more. What was worse—the pain I had caused everyone by lying, or the pain I had caused them with my "honesty"? Was it worse for my children now that their father was overseas, living as a gay man? Was deceiving them better or worse than breaking up their family in order to attempt living a life of truth? Any way I looked at it, I was embittered by guilt and angst.

I lived in a fog at the time, painfully surviving each day rather than living it. So little was clear to me. Not for a minute did I miss living as a fraud. I grieved for all the time I had wasted, for the many unfulfilled and tainted moments that defined the first twenty years of my journey—moments that became my history and could never be relived or reclaimed. And yet, I truly missed my family, Israel, and the religious life I had left behind.

On one particularly foggy day, I saw a homeless man on the subway, dirty, dazed, and showing signs of dementia. I was petrified of becoming this man—a fate that seemed all too possible. I didn't yet know that there was a way out of this madness, this prison, this state of confinement.

I decided I needed to do something for my soul, even though I convinced myself that nothing in New York could approach the spiritual depth of what I had experienced in Israel. I needed to find a synagogue that would not exclude me for being gay, even if homosexuality was not my truth. Congregation Beit Simchat Torah (CBST) advertised itself as a progressive synagogue that welcomed "gay men, lesbians, bisexuals, transgender, queer, and straight individuals and families." Although it was only later that I understood what the term transgender meant, this seemed an apt community to attempt to join. After not having been to a Friday night service for the better part of a year, I longed for this. I also craved community.

I had no idea what to expect. After having been Orthodox for close to twenty years, I had no context within which to imagine what I would encounter. However, my combined state of loneliness, thirst for spiritual expression, guilt over both the past and the present, and general state of depression pushed me to finally attend a Shabbat service.

My experience ranged from one end of the emotional spectrum to the other. Just about everyone welcomed me warmly. Everyone appeared to be happy and at peace. Initially, I imagined what it would be like to attend regularly and become a member of this community. With ease and joy, I fantasized all types of traditional and spiritually evocative experiences, in the backdrop of being in community. Maybe this would provide me a way back to my own Jewish identity, an identity that was withering away with the passing of each Shabbat. "I can do this," I said to myself. I felt optimistic and encouraged. But I hadn't yet been in the synagogue for ten minutes. Oh, how desperation can exaggerate and suggest scenarios that are beyond the grasp of reality.

Eventually, reality began to set in. I sat alone during the service. I tried to daven, to engage in spiritual prayer, the way I was taught and felt comfortable with. The service seemed to be an afterthought, almost in the background of what appeared to arouse much more passion and devotion—lots of chatter, flirting, and laughter. I sighed. I was glad for "them" that "they" had a synagogue to attend, a safe space where they clearly felt comfortable and included rather than excluded. But as with Orthodox synagogues, this space was intended for a specific audience. Clearly, I was not part of this group. This was always my challenge. How could I feel included in any group if I was not honest with myself?

My experience at CBST lacked so much—spiritual passion, vibrancy, depth, and the presence of God! But above all else, it was the social hour that was off-putting for me. It was then that I saw the sadness, loneliness, and desperate need of the congregants to be accepted into a community. The hidden pain behind everyone's masks of smiles and laughter was too much to bear. It drove me away, and I never returned.

These were dark years. Any moments of relief or happiness were short lived, doused by pangs of guilt for causing my family incredible hardship and confusion. I felt as though I had just fallen over the edge of a cliff, barely able to hold on. I was not even sure what I was trying to hold. A prayer for redemption, perhaps? A glimmer of hope for a future of honest living? A sign of encouragement to live an authentic life? I prayed for a glimmer of hope, a sign of encouragement. But I was quickly losing my grip.

Chapter 25

LOSING MY GRIP

Desperate to connect to anyone and anything that resembled life, I clung to those around me while I withered away from within. My new life honored the flesh rather than the soul. Immediate gratification reigned, but it was painfully limiting, its pleasures short lived.

The popular slogan of the day claimed, "It's not how you feel, but rather how you look." The sentiment made me cringe. The pressure to look a certain way in order to fit in and be accepted reminded me too much of my experience in Crown Heights. I was never sure who outdid the other in the battle to win me over—the chassidim or the gays—permeated as both cultures were with the fierce intent to claim my soul.

I did not belong in either community. Heterosexual, ultra-Orthodox Chassidic men and gay, ultra-progressive men had more in common than either group would ever care to admit. Community pressure, peer pressure, and societal pressure all collaborated against my well-being. In both environments, I wished I had the courage to live a life true to myself, my life, rather than the life others expected of me.

My mind was flooded with memories of having been spiritually awakened in 1971, and the years that followed. Where did they go? How did I arrive at such a spiritually hollow and empty place? My soul longed for nourishment. At the time, though, I believed that the source of my soul's nourishment was one that had cast me out. Traditionally observant Jews intentionally excluded me and made me feel unwelcome.

I was working for a travel agency in Manhattan that specialized in trips to Israel. Every day I went to the office wearing tight jeans, a tight shirt, and a haircut that messaged to everyone which club I belonged to. Of course, no kippah, no beard, no traditional Jewish garb. If my haircut left anyone wondering what lifestyle I adopted, my uniform did not.

One day at work I heard commotion outside my office. Colleagues, both Israeli and American, were passionately exclaiming to one another, "Reb Shlomo is here, Rabbi Carlebach is here, Reb Shlomo is here!" Evidently, he would come to this office from time to time to purchase tickets for his many trips to Israel.

It was now 1994. We had not seen each other since my divorce, and obviously much about me had changed—at least on the outside. What happened next may have meant more to me than our first encounter in 1971, when he made me feel that my life actually possessed intrinsic value and that it mattered.

I was petrified that my very first rebbe would question me and make me feel even more ashamed than I already was. A part of me wanted to run away before he got a glimpse of me. I used to sit with him and learn how to be close to God, close to my own spiritual center, and to others. And look at me now! I felt so filthy, so dirty, so cowardly.

And then it happened. Reb Shlomo took one look at me, and his smile became larger than life itself, his eyes popped out of his head. He came right over to me, hugged me, called me Yaakov, the Hebrew name I had stopped using when I left Israel, and said, "Holy brother, holy brother, gevaldt—amazing, you are helping send fellow Jewish brothers and sisters to Israel! Gevaldt."

That day stood out in my journey. I never forgot it. I never want to forget it. I was losing my grip, and he helped me hang on. He helped me remember who I really was.

Later that fateful day, I did something I had not done for a long time. I looked up to the heavens and into myself, and I begged God for a sign, something to help me pull myself up from the abyss of a totally hedonistic way of life.

And the sign appeared! It was a modern-day miracle. I would regularly buy a publication that catered to the New York gay and lesbian communities. The articles were boring at best, occasionally offensive, and yet, I continued to buy the magazine month after month. That day I sat down in Bryant Park with the newest edition of the Advocate. Staring at me, for the first time in my life, was an article about someone like me!

It was an interview with a woman in her fifties who knew from a very early age that she was born female but held captive in a male body. For the first fifty years of her life, she passionately, pathetically attempted to live as a man. She married, her wife gave birth to a boy and then a girl, she became a CEO for a very successful company and lived "the good life"—a luxury apartment on the upper East Side, vacations galore, private schools for her children, membership in the most coveted private clubs, and more.

My eyes were glued to the page, and time stood still as I read on. After her two children graduated from college and she was able to ensure financial security for her wife, she made her big announcement. She told the truth. She freed herself from her prison. She came clean with her true self. She announced she was going to undergo full, complete gender transition, leading up to the necessary surgery that would fix her body. Finally, her body and soul would be able to reside together as one, complementing each other instead of being at war with each other.

For the first time, I learned the definitions for terms like transgender, transsexual, gender transition, gender identity disorder, gender dysphoria, hormone replacement therapy (HRT), and sexual reassignment surgery (SRS), otherwise known as genital reconstruction surgery (GRS).

Right then and there, on a bench in Bryant Park, I knew I was no longer condemned to a life in prison, to a madhouse, to the demons that took possession of my mind, heart, and soul. There was a way out! This was my path to a life of real authentic living.

Of course, at that moment I was not yet ready to begin my physical transition, but I now had possession of two very important insights. First, I was not the only person on the planet suffering from this nightmare of being born one gender but held captive by the body of another. Second, and perhaps more important, I now knew that one day I would be freed.

From that day on, I started allowing my natural female persona to find expression instead of keeping it hostage deep down inside. While not all gay couples adopt stereotypically masculine and feminine roles in their relationships, I wanted to date only men who clearly saw the feminine in me. And for me, this took no effort. I was beginning to feel lighter.

One day I was in a car, as the passenger, with Dave, a man I had been dating for a few months. We went on a road trip for a long weekend. We were talking, and all of a sudden he said to me, "Do you have to sit that way?" I replied, "What way?" With harsh judgment, he answered, "You sit just like a girl." While not having an inkling what that meant, for the first time in my life I said, "Yep! This is how I am comfortable, and this is how I will sit." We broke up right after the road trip. But for the first time, the very first time, I embraced myself without apologies, excuses, or shame.

Outwardly, it appeared to the world that I was losing my grip on my soul, on my spiritual center, on my Jewish identity. Inwardly, I knew that this was the very beginning of my eventual return. It would take a few more years, but I would only strengthen my grip on reality from here on out.

Many times I have wondered what would have happened if I had not met my rebbe that day at work and if I had not read that article in the Advocate—two pivotal moments, two pivotal stepping-stones in my journey. My answer is always the same. I say to myself, "But I did. In fact, I did."

Chapter 26

YOU WANT TO BE MY WIFE!

By 1997, I felt I had to leave New York. The winters in Manhattan were as brutal as my life. The cold, blistery, damp winds blew right through me and chilled me to the bone. These unkind and unforgiving winds embittered my plight, especially when walking "home" to my empty, void-of-life apartment in the dark after work. I was always cold during those cruel winters, both physically and emotionally. I simply could not warm up. The filthy blackish snow mirrored back to me my own inner filth. Snow was supposed to be white and clean and beautiful. I was supposed to look beautiful. The rippled, uneven, icy sidewalks made walking treacherous, and my own life's path seemed equally unsafe.

Shortly before I left New York for San Francisco, my maternal grandmother passed away. We had a very close relationship, and I always sensed that she knew I was more her granddaughter than her grandson. I regretted not ever having told her who I really was, but then again, how could I have? Until recently, I wouldn't have been able to articulate my feelings with the right words. I believe that she would have supported me from her place of endless love and compassion, but it was too late. Now all I could do was look up and hope that, from her place in the world of truth, she would encourage me to taste honest living, and that from my place, in the world of deception, I would hear it. Eventually, I did.

I knew when I left New York that it would finally be for good. Even though my journey had brought me back to New York several times, now I strongly sensed that it would not happen again. And it has not. With less than a few people to say good-bye to, I left and have not looked back since. Intuitively, I sensed that going west would one day lead me back home to the east—the far east. Something momentous was awaiting me "out west." I was now venturing forth to claim it.

I moved to San Francisco in 1997 and lived downtown in the South of Market (SOMA) area. Within a month of my arrival, I met Richard. Even before we first said hello, at first glance, he claimed a piece of my heart. Until today, that piece remains with him. Even if it were possible, I would not ask for it in return. It was and remains to this day the most precious gift I could ever have given him. And that does not begin to express the gratitude I have for what he gave me. He has remained one of the dearest friends in my life.

Aside from being a brilliant professor and researcher, charismatic, incredibly handsome, and manly, he had a palpable spiritual awareness. His awareness of his own soul and the souls of others around him captivated me. In his first email to me, shortly after having met, he asked, "How is your soul?" No one had ever asked me about my soul. No one! We both enhanced our growing connection with lively and challenging spiritually directed discussions and experiences together.

Our relationship took on the complexity of a fine wine. We did everything together. We ate in fine restaurants, attended the ballet, went to dance clubs, hosted dinners, went to the beach and to Disneyland. In each of these experiences, we fascinated each other by deeply living every moment in time.

My background was in learning and teaching Torah-based mystical thought, and his experience was with the spiritual teachings of Catholicism. Our discussions were lively and charged. We talked a lot about the Jewish mystical idea of tikkun, the healing of the soul on a personal level and the fixing of the world on a global level.

I began to sense that my own personal tikkun meant finding harmony in what I once thought was absolutely incompatible. My talks with Richard about tikkun helped me understand my conflicted life in a new way. Until now, I had believed my demons were gender identity confusion and the passionate desire to live a spiritual life within the Jewish tradition that conflicted with it. But now, I began to realize that I was not in fact suffering from gender identity confusion. I had known my whole life that I was a woman. Likewise, my passionate desire to live a spiritual life within the Jewish tradition never really conflicted with the solution to this state of temporary insanity. That was my own false illusion. My strongest inner demon was buying into this myth at all. It was the myth that denied me both my true gender and my Jewish identity. My demons were actually fear, shame, and the worship of public opinion. Living a life of deception, lies, and falsehood was fodder for the demon of false illusion. With

Richard, I encountered a breakthrough in my own sense of self.

When he learned that I had not made a seder, the Passover meal with the associated rituals, since 1991, Richard insisted I organize one for the two of us and eight other friends. I organized and led both the rituals with their spiritual meanings and the traditional festive meal. That seder was undoubtedly my first real Passover. As the assorted guests, Jewish and Gentile, straight and gay/lesbian, took turns recounting the biblical narrative of the Hebrews' freedom from slavery, I couldn't help but sense a similar movement beginning to unfold in my own life.

While he was helping pave the way for my spiritual rebirth, Richard also managed to see my feminine side more than anyone else in my past. Effortlessly, Richard simply assumed the stereotypical role of the man. He was clearly in charge, protective, and responsible for leading us on the path that we walked together. This way, I was free to express the more sensitive side of myself. When I grew up, my mother voiced very few criticisms to me. I always tried to make her proud and be "a good boy." However, the one thing she said all too often, with disapproval, was "You are too sensitive!" What she really meant to say was "You are too sensitive for a boy."

Richard valued my sensitive and gentle personality. He liked how I accommodated his wishes with a big smile, and he loved my nurturing nature. I always made sure he felt completely at home in my house. He created a safe space for me to begin to naturally express my inner female self, which was now almost fifty years old and screaming for expression. And the kind of female I felt I typified was the type of personality that he found attractive and compatible with his own.

I wondered at times where this relationship would lead. Here we were, outwardly both male, and yet, the strong growing connection between us was rife with opposing energies—male/female, masculine/feminine, protector/nurturer. Oddly enough, we never once discussed our dynamic in this way. I never opened my closet door and fully came out to him as a transgendered woman. Was I afraid? Perhaps I wasn't ready yet. Maybe I just never felt the need. But Richard knew me very well.

By early 2000, he said he had something very serious to discuss with me. I had been feeling tension for a few months but was clueless as to why. Richard gently told me he wanted to break up with me. He could not continue our relationship. I was devastated. My entire world at that time revolved around him. In no way could I bear the thought that this dependence was unhealthy, so I did what I do best with any insights into self-awareness that I don't like. I denied it.

He wanted to explain why he was breaking up with me and cautioned me greatly. He told me that he knew I would throw a temper tantrum, deny the truth of what he was going to say, and that I would try to convince him of my own version of a contrived truth. He looked at me and with love, only with love, he said, "What you want is wonderful. It's a beautiful dream. But it's your dream and not mine. There is absolutely nothing wrong with what you want, but it's not what I want." I replied, with tears in my eyes, voice quivering, stomach upset, "OK! OK! OK! What do you think I want?"

With complete clarity, he looked into my eyes and said, "You want to be my wife. I am gay, and I don't want a wife. Please listen to me and believe me that I know this is what you want. For your own good, for your own well-being, for your own tikkun, do what you need to do to become who you really are! And I will always be there supporting you as your loving friend."

As he predicted, I threw an absolute fit. I denied what he said was true. I made up some ridiculous reply about how I liked being more like the woman but I am still a man and of course I did not want to be his wife. He looked at me again, into my eyes, and lovingly said, "It's time you be honest with yourself. Do what you must for your tikkun." He hugged me and left.

I sat there in tears, not because I thought what he said was not true, but because I knew he was right. He had looked into my eyes, the gateway to my soul, and told me the truth. Now I had to look at myself and do the same. I needed to admit that in fact, yes, I wanted to be Richard's wife.

* * *

Thirteen years later, in 2013, I came back to San Francisco for a meeting. I contacted Richard, with whom I had remained in touch for the past thirteen years, and we met for lunch.

Over lunch I told him about writing my memoir, about how my life had changed and how I now felt healed and grateful. I then recounted the episode of our breakup. I thanked him for being the first person in my life who, from a place of love, cared enough about me to tell me the truth about myself. I expressed eternal gratitude to him.

He then told me something I had never known. He told me how difficult this had been for him. Not so much telling me the truth, but experiencing the tension I was feeling during those months prior to the breakup. He realized then that something was not right with us, and notwithstanding his higher-than-average intelligence, he could not figure it out. For months, he reviewed everything about our relationship over and over again, but he just could not understand what was wrong. One day he suddenly realized what was underlying his misgivings. He realized that I was a woman!

Chapter 27

THE DARKEST DAY IN MY LIFE

I awoke on the morning of July 3, 2001, to my fiftieth birthday. It was the loneliest, darkest, and most disconnecting day in my life. Other than my mother, I don't recall anyone else in my family calling me to wish me a happy birthday. I had alienated them all by now. On the fiftieth anniversary of my coming into the world, I could not even muster up the energy to congratulate myself. What I longed for had evaded me. I envisioned what it would have been like to wake up feeling grateful and blessed for having reached this milestone. I envisioned what it would have been like to celebrate this special day. I envisioned what others I know may have felt when they awoke on their fiftieth birthdays. For me, though, there was no gratitude, no feeling blessed, and no celebration.

The pangs of utter loneliness and feelings of barely surviving a life journey steeped in darkness and plagued by despair are what greeted me in a cruel embrace.And from such a dark place of decay, from an almost deathlike existence, came a sudden revelation. All I could do on my fiftieth birthday was to resolve to make a change. There I was, previously an Orthodox Jew, a spiritual leader, facing an identity crisis that had forced me to leave the very life that provided my sustenance and yet pushed me further and further away from living an honest one. This crisis brought me face-to-face with every single decision I had made in my life up until that very moment in time, most of them having been from a place of dishonesty and deception.

Realizing that every second I continued to breathe air into my male body was a lie, I understood that I must finally make a choice: I could just stop breathing, or I could own my gender identity issues and start over. I could make the decision to discover what it would take to become the woman I always knew I was meant to be, destined to be. And I did in fact make that decision. Continuing with the lie that was my life was no longer an option. I was exhausted. I was drained. The daily struggle of living that lie had pulled me apart. I had hit my own spiritual and emotional "rock bottom."

On my fortieth birthday, I had decided that I could no longer continue living a traditional Torah-based life. This decision was heart wrenching and forced me to uproot every aspect of my life that was inauthentic—my religiously observant lifestyle in Jerusalem, my livelihood as an outreach educator to students and tourists, my relationships with my wife and children, multitudes of neighbors, friends, and professional associates. Even worse, this decision plunged me into a place of painful loneliness, despair, and tremendous guilt for the hurt I caused my family.

A part of me wished to go back home to Israel. A part of me desired to return to Jewish spiritual living. I missed Jewish community and Torah observance. But I knew that if someday I were to return, I could return only in truth. And this meant I could return only as a woman. I was not sure if living my life as a woman would provide me a path back to Judaism, but it was clear that I could never return as a man.

So now, on my fiftieth birthday, right then, I took a "leap of faith," catapulting past the strangling, suffocating demons wringing the life out of me. At that very moment, I embarked on my gender transition journey, not knowing where it would take me, what I would have to leave behind, or what I would need to reclaim from my past in order to be truly whole. By trying to be someone else and by trying to live someone else's life for all those years, my gender dysphoria had distanced me from my relationship with God, the one source of strength and nourishment I had always counted on to keep me centered and spiritually alive.

On my fiftieth birthday, I gave myself the ultimate gift: the decision to begin living the truth. I embraced this gift with an open and broken heart, and have never let go since. This decision was so huge, so momentous, that all I could do was make it and embrace it.

PART FIVE

LETTING GO AND TRUSTING
2001–2005

Chapter 28

CALLING OUT IN ANGUISH

After 210 years of the Hebrews' enslavement to the Egyptians, they cried out to God for help. That pivotal moment in Jewish history gave birth to the dawn of redemption from bitter slavery to sweet freedom:

...and the Children of Israel groaned because of being enslaved, and they cried out. Their outcry from their enslavement ascended to God. God heard their moaning. (Exodus 2:23–24)

After fifty years of being enslaved to my own inner Egyptian taskmasters, I likewise called out to God. In anguish I groaned, and God heard me. From a place of utter helplessness and desperation, I cried out to God. This was the pivotal moment in my life, the dawn of my own personal redemption.

For fifty years I attempted to control my life. I became a figment of other people's imaginations. It was as if "I" the dreamer and the "me" in the dream took on two different lives. A fissure between the two defined my life. I became other than what I was. The more I tried to control my life, the more it spun out of control. The decision to once and for all live a life of truth forced me to confront this painful irony. My futile efforts to control that which I could not left me embittered and worn out, and yet ripe and ready for something new. Like a seed planted in the cold, dark earth, from a place of such inner decay, I too could germinate and blossom. To do this, I needed to surrender my false illusion of control. I needed to live my life instead of attempting in vain to control it. To whom do I surrender? To the One who controls, but of course! To God. This may have been my first authentic religious experience with God. No more deals. No more manipulations. No more conditional agreements. My personal redemption meant that I would follow instead of lead.

Living in a dreamlike state brought with it unexpected revelations and surprises. By losing myself to a force infinitely greater than me, in my own cold and lonely night, I began to sprout. I began to see parts of myself that had remained hidden my whole life, suddenly exposed to all in the light of day. I began to realize that all along I had possessed the secret to living a life of authenticity. What a jewel! I awoke from this dark sleep to sense God in my life. I was no longer alone! Unbeknownst to me until now, I had possessed the secret of prayer all along. I began talking to God, crying to God, beseeching God, and pleading with God for direction toward sincere living.

I marveled when I began to experience God dwelling within me, always accessible. All I needed to do was gently move out of my own way, allowing Him space to dwell and to reveal Himself to me. From this space, God reached His guiding hand out to me and invited me to hold on, to cleave, and to never let go. This acceptance and surrender meant admitting that my "self" was no longer, and never was, the master of the house. I gave up what was and became open to what may be. I gave up the lie of my life and became open to the possibility of living the truth. Discovering and feeling HaShem within me inspired my new lifetime venture.

Living my life in truth meant acknowledging the secret of real living as I now understood it. It meant calling out and calling within, in prayer, to the Force that listens and brings redemption, compassion, and unconditional love to the relationship. I collided with the toxic, self-destructive part of myself, my ego, as I blindly arrived in darkness, groping with no direction in the night of my life. I came out of this crash invigorated, encouraged, and loved by a very different part of myself, my soul—that piece of God within me.

In Jewish tradition, the process of returning home to one's true self, to the part of oneself that outlives life itself, to the presence of HaShem within, is referred to as teshuva—returning. During the summer of 2001, at the age of fifty, I began my teshuva process in earnest. For the first time in my life, I truly prayed and begged God to bring me home to Him, to myself, to the ultimate truth.

A startling insight became apparent to me as I began to walk down the path of teshuva. As I held on to God's guiding hand, as I followed the Leader, I suddenly realized what else I needed to do for this journey to succeed. Surrendering control, holding on to God's hand, and being in conversation, while huge and momentous for me, would not suffice. The path of walking with God meant that I must be willing to sacrifice everything and anything in order to honestly partake of it.

In the Bible, God tested Abraham in a way that would cause even the strongest believers to crumble and fall apart—

or perhaps not. Abraham was commanded, expected, and required to offer up his beloved son Isaac on the altar as a human child sacrifice. This collided with and contradicted every aspect of how Abraham had come to encounter and know God, and yet, he enthusiastically rose to the occasion. At the very last moment, God prevented Abraham from going through with the slaughtering of his beloved son. He then told Abraham:

By Myself I swear—the word of HaShem—that because you have done this thing, and have not withheld your son, your only one, that I shall surely bless you… (Genesis 22:16–17)

I knew I needed to be willing to sacrifice that which was most precious to me for this journey to be real. I sought God's blessing, I needed God's blessing to go further on my journey. My gender transition could never be right without God's blessing, guidance, and direction. I simply could not imagine taking the next step, and each one after that, alone. As God's love and compassion is unconditional, I was required to commit myself unconditionally to being in this relationship. No price would be too high to live a life of dignity and truth.

For fifty years, in one way or another, I talked the talk. I whined, I cried, I lied, I complained, I manipulated myself and others, and I felt victimized by the circumstances into which I was born. I believed that I would do anything that would grant me God's blessing to taste a moment of authentic, honest, clean living. It was now time to walk the walk. I needed to take responsibility for my fiftieth-birthday decision and for my part in my own life journey.

I began by surrendering and letting go of the false illusion that I actually controlled my journey. To be decisive now meant calling out in anguish, in horrific pain, for HaShem to lead me, with no conditions. Venturing forth into the completely unknown future required that I learn to trust God. No sacrifice was greater than what I had already sacrificed for fifty years—my self-respect, dignity, self-esteem, and my very soul, the image of God in which I was created.

I never wanted to be anyone other than me, but I never knew what price I would pay to in fact become myself. And yet, as I called out to God in anguish, I was ready to sacrifice whatever God deemed necessary for my redemption.

Chapter 29

WHAT IS BEING ASKED OF ME?

Unplanned, unexpected, and unannounced, God's leading hand brought me to Palm Springs, CA, in 2002. There, I came into contact with a friend whom I had originally met in Tzfat in 1977 and with whom I had last reconnected in Jerusalem in 1985. We had not seen each other since I left Jerusalem in 1991. Perched on the first stepping-stone of my gender transition journey, I clearly did not appear the way she remembered me when I wore the disguise of an Orthodox Chassidic male in Jerusalem. However, she looked exactly as I remembered her eleven years earlier. To the naïve onlooker, we must have appeared out of place with each other. But our souls had been deeply connected for years, and we effortlessly picked up from where we left off in Jerusalem.

We went for a long walk away from the noise of the commercial downtown area. We were able to actively listen to each other and cherish this unexpected shared moment in time. With focused intent, we heard each other speak. With excitement, but omitting details, I began to describe how I was beginning my journey to authentic living. With equal excitement, and with no shortage of details, she told me all about her life in California: Her marriage, large family, community work, and teaching, all under the umbrella of continuing to live a Torah-based Jewish life, kept her extremely busy and fulfilled with a sense of purpose.

As different as our outer lives were, the starkest contrast between us was internal. In a candid yet soft and gentle tone, almost in an obvious, matter-of-fact way, she shared an insight with me that became the underlying theme of my gender transition journey. She said to me, "The main difference between you and me at this juncture in our lives is that you are doing exactly what you want to do, and I am doing exactly what I believe God wants me to do. Your life answers the question 'What do I want, and what do I want of God?' My life answers the question 'What does God want, and what does God want of me?'"

A flash of enlightenment engulfed me. Suddenly, my blockage with God became crystal clear. While we eventually said our good-byes and wished each other well, her words remained with me. They made an indelible permanent impression on my soul and on my path in returning to a Torah-based way of life.

I now realized that I needed to take one more essential step for my gender transition journey to work, to heal me, and to be right. Although I was certain that I needed to do this, that God would guide and bless me through the transition, and that I was willing to sacrifice everything in order to live a life of truth, there still remained one more essential step. I now felt compelled to inquire of God if in fact this was what He wanted of me. Before beginning a gender transition journey,

I needed to transition my sense of being from that of creator to that of created being. I understood that as a created being, my life would have meaning only relative to that which God designed for me when creating me. As my Maker, God defined for me my intrinsic value. Any sense of worth had to be aligned with the purpose assigned to me by God.

In other words, living a life of authenticity could be accomplished only if what made it authentic was God's will for me.

This spiritual mind-set, a transition in and of itself, brought my teshuva journey to a new level. My gender transition journey needed to be in alignment with, in harmony with, and a direct response to my spiritual journey of returning home to God and to my spiritual center. After all, my soul was the epicenter of pure, pristine truth.

So, now I spent the next few months in dialogue with God, meditating and reflecting, and asking if in fact this was what God wanted of me. And if my gender transition was not what God wanted of me, then what did He want of me? My broken life, my broken heart, my broken relationships with myself, family, and community desperately needed tikkun. My soul needed tikkun.

I once and for all unconditionally pledged my loyalty and commitment to my relationship with HaShem. All I could ask for now was to be shown the path on which I was destined to walk. If it meant gender transition, so be it, and if not, equally so be it. I prayed hard for only one thing—clarity of what God was asking of me. If I sensed God's presence on my journey, I would know the journey was meant to be. If I sensed God's presence on my journey, I knew that I had nothing to fear or doubt. If I sensed God's presence on my journey, I would never ever be alone, lonely, or disconnected again.

For the past twenty-one years, I had convinced myself that healing my gender identity disorder was in conflict with my passionate desire to live a spiritual life within the Jewish tradition. I now realized that this was a total falsehood. In fact, I would never truly heal my gender identity disorder if it were to be separate from living a spiritual life within the Jewish tradition. Instead of the two paths going in opposite, incompatible directions, they needed to converge and become one if this was what God destined for me.

For the first time in my life, I remained completely open to being led to the answer to a question I feared asking for fifty-one years: God, as my Creator, as Your creation, what are You asking of me?

Chapter 30

PLUNGING INTO THE SEA

I met David in 2002, and within a few months he invited me to move into his home in Colorado Springs. He sought a partner who enjoyed playing the role of a 1950s housewife. It seemed we were destined for each other. I would be responsible for the home: cooking, cleaning, shopping, and supervising his two children from his previous marriage when they would sleep over. In essence, I became their stepmother. After helping raise my own six children, I knew both intuitively and experientially how to do this. In return, I would be financially and emotionally supported and we would "live happily ever after." As much as a man could treat another man as a woman, David succeeded in behaving that way toward me. I even managed to forget, from time to time, that my female soul was still inhabiting a male body.

I loved it. This experience made me feel like my mother's daughter at long last. I would call her up for recipe suggestions and other advice on how to run a home. She was the expert in homemaking and child rearing, and I had always looked up to her as the best role model a daughter could ever hope for. This whole scenario was almost too good to be true.

With each passing day, I effortlessly adopted a blossoming female persona. My soul found all the essential nutrients for proper growth in the environment I came to call my new home. I felt remarkably real, honest, and clean. I met David in a way that could best be described by the nonbeliever as coincidental, but it was clear to me that HaShem sent David into my life as an expression of His Divine personal intervention. David encouraged me to express my Jewish identity in any way that I wished, confirming that my gender transition journey would help me return to my own spirituality, steeped in traditional Torah Judaism.

Most of my newly made acquaintances were women, and for the first time in my life, other than when I taught in the all-girls school in Tzfat in 1977, I felt I was with my own kind. Nothing felt contrived or forced. I felt so comfortable, so relaxed, so "me." This brought incredible relief to the chronic pain of disconnection I suffered during the many nightmarish years I was forced to socialize exclusively with males.

Above all this, I experienced a moment of such exquisite clarity that it seemed absolutely prophetic. I was sitting with a group of friends. Suddenly, one of the women said she wanted to share an important decision with all of us. In as calm and clear way as possible, she explained to us that she was actually a male who was held captive by her female body. Her time to begin her gender transition journey had arrived. The next immediate step lay before her. She asked us to call her Mark. As Mark, my friend hoped we would bless and support him on this journey of healing.

One week after the Hebrews were freed from Egypt, they found themselves in the most challenging of situations. In front of them was the deep, murky, turbulent Sea of Reeds. On either side of them were wild animals. Pursuing them from behind was the united and well-organized Egyptian army. Terrified, they cried out to God. Some cried out in prayer for salvation and Divine help. Some cried out with regret that they were ever freed, claiming, "Were there no graves in Egypt that You took us to die in the wilderness?" (Genesis 14:11). This group wanted to surrender. A third group wanted to fight the Egyptians to the end. Out of desperation and panic, a fourth group suggested suicide.

All four responses are within our grasp of understanding. Any one of us would agree that if we ourselves had been there, or in a similar situation, we very well would have reacted in one of these four ways ourselves. Moses cried out to God, frustrated, not knowing what to do. "HaShem said to Moses, 'Why do you cry out to Me? Speak to the Children of Israel and let them journey ahead'" (Genesis 14:15). Basically, God commanded that all the prayers and complaints, the calls to bear arms and to give in to despair, stop immediately. It was time! The time had arrived for the people to demonstrate their readiness to put their lives in danger in obedience to God by plunging into the water. That degree of faith would earn them the miracle of the Splitting of the Sea. In that very moment, God commanded each of the Children of Israel to go forward into the unknown future.

So, too, my time had come. No more praying, no more turning back in surrender and regret, no more fighting, and surely no more despair. The time to plunge into my unclear future, into my own dark and murky sea, had arrived. I had no idea whether my personal sea would split, revealing all. But I did know that it was time to take action. For the first time ever, I realized that if I were to have any real chance of living authentically, if my life were to have intrinsic meaning and value, I had to jump in and discover my own destiny and future. I had no idea what would happen next, but I was finally ready to jump.

As I sat there and absorbed what Mark said on that fateful day, I heard HaShem say to me, "Jump in. Plunge in. Dive in. No more living like a woman held captive in a male body. Jump into your future! Plunge into your own life! Claim the life I have destined for you with dignity, gratitude, and grace!"

Suddenly I stood up and exclaimed, "Me too! Only I am going in the other direction." Mark looked at me, and gasped, and rejoiced. He hugged me and said, "Thank God. We were all waiting for you to begin your journey as well." This was my moment. The burden of over fifty years of living other people's lives, of catering to other people's expectations of me, of being immersed in deception and lies, gently disappeared. In that one moment, I unloaded tons of anxiety, low self-esteem, self-hatred, the sense of being victimized, and the feeling of being disconnected from me, from the world, and from God. I cried out in joy, in celebration, in closeness. I was beginning in earnest the return to the real me, and to the part of God within me.

HaShem had made it clear what was being asked of me. Loud and clear. And as with my own ancestors, I was prepared to sacrifice whatever I had to in order to obey God's plan for me. Little did I know how my own sea would so eloquently and gracefully split, allowing me easy passage to "the other side," where I would be able to witness my own inner demons drown and die forever.

Chapter 31

AND THE HEALING BEGINS

It was at this point that David and I broke up. While he respected and even supported the next chapter in my life journey, he could not accompany me any further. I listened to him, I heard him, I understood him, and I knew he was right. Without protest, denials of any kind, or even a tear, I parted from him and began to embrace my own life. This was my own personal journey, and I needed to walk on the path accompanied only by God.

I called Richard, and he blessed me, supported me, and lovingly encouraged me to move ahead.

That year, 2004, so much seemed to happen so fast, and yet, I never felt pressured to race ahead of myself. There is no clear instruction manual on how to transition one's body from one end of the gender spectrum to the other. Rather, it was an experiment in learning to trust my own intuition. Before moving from one stepping-stone to the next, I gave myself time to consider my next move. I considered the consequences, both to myself and to those around me. One very important point remained clear to me from the outset of my gender transition journey through its completion: I believed this was God's will, God's plan, and God's way of healing for me. Therefore, I could transition only with dignity, patience, and respect—both for me and for others. I felt myself transitioning not only into a complete woman, but into a gentle, kind, and compassionate human being. These were traits I had always wanted to cultivate and exemplify, but they had gotten lost in my struggle to survive. No longer fighting to survive, no longer simply reacting to life, I was now able to honor life and be proactive about living. With each step, I meditated and sought HaShem's guidance and presence. When I did not sense HaShem's presence, I waited until I did.

After attending a few informational seminars, I began hormone replacement therapy (HRT). My doctor specialized in HRT for women—both genetically born and transgendered. She explained to me that my regiment was similar to that prescribed for a woman at the start of menopause. At first I experienced hot flashes—suddenly breaking into a sweat in the middle of the cold Colorado winter. I became overly sensitive to myself and to others. For no apparent reason, I would suddenly find myself crying, having no prior experience or context within which to relate these highly emotionally charged moments. After a period of adjustment, I thankfully began to feel a calm inside me that I had never experienced before. My body and brain welcomed estrogen with relief and gratitude. At the same time, testosterone, the raging wild demon that had sought to destroy me for the past forty years, began to weaken its vicious hold on me. I felt balanced and calm and, oddly, empowered and strong.

I worked for Starbucks at the time, and I spoke to upper management about my decision. I wanted to strategize with them how to best discuss my decision with our staff, and if necessary with our customer base. I worked in a typically busy Starbucks store, surrounded by all kinds of people. I knew I must find a way to gently ease my own changes into this highly populated customer base as well. My store manager and district manager confessed ignorance to the gender transition journey. However, they did not hesitate to express their respect and support. In fact, the Rocky Mountain regional director personally visited me and told me in no uncertain terms that in the capacity of a Starbucks partner, if he could not extend complete support to me, he had no right representing the company on the regional level. For the first time in my life, the real me was acknowledged and appreciated. Not only was Starbucks respectful and supportive, but they were able to continue to evaluate my professional performance without bias, and I soon received a promotion into the store management training program.

I began wearing female attire, and several girlfriends eagerly took me shopping and helped me choose styles, colors, textures, and outfits that met my needs, while being age appropriate and in good taste. A new world opened up to me. Shopping! Shoes, makeup, accessories, basics, casual, dressy. Every exciting step felt normal and correct. I no longer felt like an imposter, sneaking into the men's changing room to try on the drab, boring costumes in which I felt forced to masquerade.

My hair grew longer and took on a definitive female look. My desire to look prettier brought me to a wig salon, and I adopted the practice of wearing wigs. As with wearing skirts and tops, dresses, hosiery and shoes, purses, and makeup, whenever I felt it was time to move forward with another step, I would wait one more day to be sure this was what God wanted for me. Once I felt that sense of approval, I went forth with God gently leading and guiding me. Never alone. Never confused. Never unsure. It was as if I looked into the world through a different pair of lenses. My view of the world was no longer smudged or hazy. It was now crystal clear. A new dimension began to characterize my vision, from one-dimensional black-and-white, flat and lifeless, to three-dimensional color, bursting with texture and expression.

I started going to salons for manicures and pedicures. For most of my life, I had seldom felt special. For most of my life, I had felt that I was denied real living. But being honest with myself, going to a salon dressed as the woman I knew myself to be, to have my nails painted and to experience being pampered, was incredibly special.

Along with HRT and dressing in feminine clothing, I also began to take voice lessons. I worked with an expert in Denver, and little by little my voice took on a more female sound. The day came when people on the other end of the phone began to refer to me as "ma'am."

I also underwent the extensive, costly, and time-consuming procedure of electrolysis to remove my facial hair. I had never felt I had a real "man's beard" until then. It seemed to take forever, and yet, with each needle's zap, I felt one step closer to having the face I was meant to have.

Each of these steps brought more and more healing to my pained and injured soul, and brought me closer to HaShem as well. I never doubted for a second that this was what I was destined to do. For the first twenty years of my Torah-observant life, not a day passed without turmoil. Since I began my transition, not a day has passed without a sense of clarity. The world began to view me as I had always seen myself. Now when I looked into the mirror, with each passing week, the mirror reflected back what I always expected to see. The irony, the profound irony, is that the "real, authentic, and genuine" me did not transition. Rather, the inner me, my soul, finally began to be revealed through my outer body. It was my body that transitioned, and not "me." My body needed to heal so it could be in harmony with my soul.

During this time, David and I went on a long weekend getaway trip. The air tickets were purchased before we broke up, and as we remained friends, we decided to follow through with our plans. On the return trip back to Colorado, as the airline attendant pushing the beverage cart reached our row, she turned to David and asked, "Sir, would you care for anything to drink?" Nothing special, nothing extraordinary, nothing but typical. She then asked me, "Ma'am, would you care for anything to drink?" I'm not sure if I ever smiled like I did at that moment. Incredibly special, incredibly extraordinary, and incredibly atypical. In time, this kind of interaction became the norm, but I cherished that moment. After all, this was the first time in my life someone had addressed me, face-to-face, by my true gender. David leaned over to me and said, "Any man that I know would be mortified and would have been embarrassed beyond words, probably wanting to go into hiding if he was addressed as ma'am. But you? You can't even imagine the grin on your face right now." I simply replied to him, "That's because I am a woman and not a man, and finally the world is beginning to acknowledge me for being who I am, rather than for being who I am not."

But it was not all glorious and exhilarating. One early morning as I was opening up the Starbucks store where I was now an assistant manager, I encountered my first confrontation. Colorado Springs is headquarters central for the right-wing Christian fundamentalist organization Focus on the Family. Many of our customers were in fact members of this organization. Even one of the women who performed electrolysis on me was a proud member, and she had difficulty reconciling my being "so nice, so sweet, so gentle" with my being a transgendered woman. However, I was the customer and she was the provider of services.

Now the tables were turned. One of our regular early morning customers, a polite and friendly woman, cornered me by the front of the store as I was setting out the milk carafes. She held my hand, looked into my eyes, and said, "How can someone as nice and respectful as you make a decision to turn your back on the Lord and go down a road of such horrible sin?" I then took her hand, looked into her eyes, and replied, "In fact, that is exactly how I lived for the first fifty years of my life. Now I am following God's wish for me, living His will, and holding on to His loving hand like never before. Only because this is what God is asking of me can I do this. And the 'this' is finally living a clean life of truth in being one with God." She was astounded. I must have shocked her. She began to cry, and then she hugged me, repeating, "I had no idea! May God bless you on your journey." She remained a loyal customer, and from that morning until I left Colorado she always inquired as to my well-being and would always conclude with "May God bless you."

Before long, I was so integrated into living and looking like the woman I am that men began to talk to me differently. I was unprepared for being patronized, and yet, in a strange way I welcomed it. Routine visits to the post office, to the supermarket, and to the car dealership brought with them a new realization of how men would begin to behave toward me. In all three instances, the male postal clerk, the male cashier, and the male auto mechanic were incredibly polite to me and yet amazingly condescending. I was dumbfounded that a man would talk to me that way, and even more caught off-guard that each one believed this was the proper way to speak to a woman. But how could I be angry? How could I be upset? They were truly treating me like a woman! I felt I had made it into the "club"—I was now a second-class citizen.

All joking aside, as with all real living, my journey not only had its many ups but brought me to some serious and painful downs. The fallout from the miraculous splitting of my own sea and my being able to walk confidently and securely to the other side on firm ground involved my family. My decision to transition shattered them. For reasons I may never grasp or be privy to, my decision to peel away the many filthy layers of deceptive living, to really live a life in alignment with God as I began returning in earnest to the Torah way of life and to being in a vibrant real relationship with God, cost me my family. It was the greatest sacrifice I could have made, but without it my sea would not have split, and I would have faced certain death by drowning.

Except for my mother, my nuclear family felt betrayed, embarrassed, humiliated, and even further distanced from me than ever before. So, as my personal healing began, my family's pain and extreme unease hit an all-time high. I was not prepared for this. While I did not expect my family to encourage and admire me for my decision to transition, I never expected their reaction. I was so immersed in the shattering of my own life that when I finally took hold of the way out of my misery, I simply could not grasp the severity of my decision from my family's point of view. I could always ask of God, why? And I did ask this of God, many times, even though I never expected an answer. Undoubtedly my biggest hurdle, my family's reaction did not inspire guilt as it had in years past. Rather, I felt compassion. I felt sadness. With each step on my journey of healing, as I began to recover from a wretched miserable life that I would wish on no one, my compassion for my family grew. Even so, their pain could not have stopped me. Their pain was unavoidable collateral damage to my healing process, and it was time for me to forge ahead with that healing.

I began to understand, to appreciate, and to experience that healing, of both body and soul, was not linear and even. The Children of Israel proceeding through the wilderness, moving closer and closer to entering their promised homeland, encountered all kinds of challenges, both internal and external. Should my journey to authentic living and healing of body and soul be any different? What was always clear was that I was undergoing healing, tikkun, as directed by my Creator and customized for my particular specific soul journey. This is what I held on to at all times.

Chapter 32

FAREWELL TO THE WRONG SIDE OF THE MECHITZA

By the spring of 2004, as my body was beginning to change, I knew I had to visit Jerusalem and say good-bye forever to the left side, the men's side, of the mechitza at the Western Wall. During the past twelve years, I returned to Israel many times. Each departure brought me pain. I never wanted to leave Israel, and each time I did it was gut wrenching and heartbreaking. Likewise, each time I visited, the Western Wall illuminated my indecisive behavior. Regardless of how expert I had become in rationalizing my irresponsible behavior away, standing before the Wall made it impossible to lie. I felt completely naked, vulnerable, and a total fraud every time I stood before that mirror made of stone.

Now the time had finally arrived to bid farewell. I didn't know when I would be returning again to Israel, but as sure as anyone can be about the future, I knew I would return only after my gender transition journey was complete. I would return only as a woman, my body externally testifying to the truth that had always existed internally.

So, that Friday night in May, I went to the Kotel. I felt the familiar cloud of agitation hover over me as I approached closer and closer to the Wall on the men's side. Since my first momentous walk in 1971, I had experienced this countless times. Each time I felt disgusted with myself. Each time I hated myself for not being honest in such a sacred space. But this time was different.

I could not pray. I did not feel any joy in being there. It was Friday night, and the peaceful Sabbath energy embodied everyone there—except me. Undoubtedly, I had encountered a new inner demon. All other inner demons paled in comparison. This one dared to rob me of the one moment that had always provided me a tiny ray of spiritual awakening and respite. I felt like more of an imposter than ever before. After all, I had already begun my transition journey, and yet, here I was again, on the wrong side of the mechitza.

But it was more than that. I was angry! So angry! Like a bolt of lightning suddenly lighting up a pitch-black forest, I became acutely aware of how angry I was with the rabbis whom I had empowered for all those years that I was a practicing Orthodox Jew. I never felt safe around them. I always felt if they knew the real me they would have done everything to push me away. In the end I pushed myself away from Orthodoxy, in large part because of them.

The only rabbis I felt safe around were Reb Shlomo Carlebach, of righteous memory, and Rabbi Menachem

Mendel Schneerson, the Chabad-Lubavitcher Rebbe, of righteous memory. Both had passed away within months of each other in 1994, so I never had the opportunity to discuss my decision to transition with either of them. I am not sure what either would have said. I sensed that each one would have responded differently, but I was sure I would have felt safe with both.

I was equally sure that I would not, could not, feel safe with any other Orthodox rabbi. Expressing my true feelings was out of the question and prohibited. All my residual rage surfaced that night. I had allowed them to push me away from Torah observance, from Jewish community, from my homeland, from Judaism, and from God.

Through my gender transition journey, I began to reclaim my Judaism. I realized that I was not created any less in the image of God than the very rabbis who made me feel less sacred than them. Now I felt compelled to let go of the "idol worship" I committed for the entire time I observed the Torah's commandments embodied in the Jewish tradition. At the Wall that night, I vowed to HaShem that I would never again worship the foreign god of rabbinical pressure to conform, to behave as a robot without spirit and integrity. I said farewell to those rabbis who claimed the right to judge me and behave toward me as God's personally appointed emissaries. For twenty years, I allowed these people to define for me the most personal, intimate relationship a human being can ever hope to experience—my relationship with God. For another ten years, I let them shut me out and push me away from my own spiritual center as well as away from God. No more. Never again!

Rage ran through my veins. In an agitated but extremely clear state, I said once and for all good-bye to much more than being a fraud masquerading as a male on the left side of the mechitza. I said good-bye to people who, out of ignorance, arrogance, and fear, would dare to hurt their fellow Jews.

I would never seek another human being's permission to live an honest life again. Only God blesses me with the breath of life, which in essence is His way of granting me permission to live. I would learn from others, yes. I would study the Jewish law from educated and God-loving and respecting rabbis, of course. I would remain open to their guidance, and be grateful to them, absolutely. However, I would not seek their permission to live my life as a Torah-observant Jewish individual, especially as a Jewish woman. That evening at the Wall, I pledged to God that it was to Him I was returning, and only to Him. My return would be to God, and not to the Orthodox rabbis who brazenly claimed to speak on behalf of Him.

As I respectfully backed away from the Wall and took my final step leading away from the men's section, my very last step, it was the part of me that was so hurt, so angry, and so desperate that I left behind. The inner rage at myself was what I truly said good-bye to that spring evening. I've never returned, either physically or emotionally, to that hurtful, horrid, and demeaning space.

Chapter 33

AND YAAKOV WRESTLED WITH THE ANGEL

Another important and necessary decision was imminent. I needed to adopt a female name. One of several conditions that the American medical community established in order for an individual to qualify as a candidate for GRS was to live an entire year as your desired gender. It is essential for individuals to be absolutely sure they are making the right decision, as obviously once one has the surgery, there is no turning back. The real-life one-year experience helps the prospective candidate be as clear as humanly possible about venturing forth into the unknown future in a new body.

My new name would message to the world that I am female, regardless of anyone's opinion or thoughts about me or around gender transition. The expectation that everyone in my life would immediately address me by my new name was unrealistic. The name of an object defines how one is to relate to it. The name of a human being even more so. The way people relate to each other, or in some cases do not relate to each other, vis-à-vis gender has permeated every single culture on every continent since the creation of Adam and Eve. So, this became a hugely significant step on my journey, and with it I needed to be absolutely clear that the time was right, that the name would resonate with me and express a deeper part of me, and that my expectations of others were seasoned with compassion, understanding, and patience.

Not only did I need to be addressed by a female name, but once chosen, every one of my legal documents needed to be changed. For this to happen, I would have to petition the county court in Colorado Springs to legally change my name due to my gender transition. Once the court legally granted my petition, I would then begin the arduous task of changing every document and account that reflected my male name for the past fifty-three years: Social Security card, driver's license, passport, credit cards, insurance policies, auto leasing agreement, bank accounts, and the list went on and on.

In most cases I was unable to legally change my gender marker from male to female, since I had not yet undergone the GRS procedure. As with every other step on this amazing and miraculous journey to becoming and living my authentic self, everything occurred in its time. In God's time. First, I needed a female name. Patience became more than a virtue; it became essential.

However, I found myself unable to choose a name. The Jewish tradition teaches that at the moment parents are about to officially and ritually name their newborn child, the spirit of Divine revelation dwells upon them, inspiring them with the clarity to accomplish this most daunting responsibility. This in fact was what I needed. I needed to be inspired. I needed God to reveal to me my new name.

I prayed hard to God for my new name. I spoke to God, and I remained open for signs, for clues, for anything that I could understand as His Divine guidance and inspiration. I knew I could not make such an important decision on my own. I needed to follow God's choice for me. I did what Jews do when they are unsure. Aside from beseeching clarity from HaShem in prayer, I looked into the Bible for inspiration and direction. I reacquainted myself with the account of Yaakov (Jacob), one of Judaism's ancient Patriarchs, when he himself underwent a profound name change:

Yaakov was left alone, and a man wrestled with him until the break of dawn…he perceived that he could not overcome him. Then he said, "Let me go, for dawn has broken." And he said, "I will not let you go unless you bless me." He said to him, "What is your name?" He replied, "Yaakov." He said, "No longer will it be said that your name is Yaakov, but Yisrael, for you have striven with the Divine and with man, and have prevailed." (Genesis 32:25–29)

I pondered this passage in Genesis. In Hebrew the word Yisrael means to struggle with God. My Hebrew name was Yaakov. I felt like I'd been struggling and striving with both the Divine and humankind most of my life, a long night indeed to be left alone and wrestle with one's inner adversary. I thought to myself, "Have I prevailed?" I imagined that perhaps I had. After all, I endured the struggle enough to remain alive and to actually ask myself such a profound question. That in and of itself messaged to me that yes, I had prevailed.

Then it happened. With an elated feeling, the cloud of uncertainty was gently lifted, and in its place I became aware of my new name. My English name, Jeffrey, transitioned into

Jessica. My Hebrew name, Yaakov, transitioned into Yiscah. The Jewish tradition believes that Yiscah, mentioned once in Genesis, was the matriarch Sara's name before she married Avraham. The oldest written record of the name Jessica is found in Shakespeare's play The Merchant of Venice, an anglicization of the name Yiscah.

I welcomed my new names with open arms, with vigor and encouragement. For so much of my life I ran, even leapt, from one stepping-stone to the next. I burnt bridges behind me, cutting off my dreadful past from what would become my equally dreadful future. Now I was clear that my gender transition journey was not a matter of running away from my past. Rather, it evolved from my past. I did not want to cut my past off from my present as I moved into the future. My past brought me to my present, which brought me comfort and some sense of living on a continuum.

My past became the seeds that sprouted forth my present. I, the ugly caterpillar, began a metamorphosis into a beautiful butterfly. The beautiful butterfly resided within the caterpillar at its birth. Yiscah dwelt within Yaakov, and after prevailing in my struggle with my spirituality and my fellow human beings, God revealed this redemptive truth to me. As well, Jessica blossomed from Jeffrey. Only after the fact, without being contrived, did I realize that retaining the same initials, both in Hebrew and in English, provided the bridge between my past and future. My new Hebrew and English names in fact honored not only my past, but my parents as well, who, with God's help, lovingly conceived me and gave me my first name.

On January 28, 2005, the El Paso County Court in the State of Colorado issued its "final decree" and officially granted my petition for my change of name. The profundity and significance of changing my name completely caught me by surprise. Yaakov/Jeffrey walked into the court that day feeling excited, a bit nervous, but sensing it was an auspicious time. Yiscah/Jessica walked out enveloped by feelings of gratitude and joy—hot, fresh, wet tears falling down my face against the background of the cold Colorado winter winds, gently rinsing away a lifetime of emotional and spiritual filth. This left me feeling cleansed and invigorated. I felt spiritually renewed as my connection with God, with my own soul, and with the world acquired a new dimension of depth and truth

PART SIX

RETURNING HOME
2005–2011

Chapter 34

THE NEWEST NEW YEAR EVER

The much anticipated day drew closer and closer. For one year I lived completely as a woman and not once incurred any major obstacles at work or in public. My employer supported me completely. All documents were changed with ease. Hormone replacement therapy, voice lessons, and electrolysis went well and in good health. Integrating into the female world came naturally to me. No moment was ever contrived or forced. In retrospect, I marveled at how much energy it took for me to unsuccessfully attempt to integrate into the male world. Journeying on my path brought me closer and closer to God and helped me return to and reclaim my Jewish identity. Each day I felt lighter and cleaner.

With my family, however, things were less than smooth. At best, out of embarrassment and confusion, some would simply have nothing to do with me. At worst, others felt abandoned and were unable to cope with my decision. It was very difficult for all of us, and it tore my family apart. Even the one person in my life who stood by me unconditionally at all times, my mother, backed away from me for a while. This saddened me beyond words. I was more than grateful when she decided to reconnect with me after having time to process my decision.

My family's varied responses, though painful, never hindered me from moving ahead. I felt strongly that HaShem commandeered my gender transition journey, and I completely trusted in His will that I execute this to completion. Did I question God? Absolutely. I questioned God about the effects this had on my family. I could not understand why my commitment to finally undergo the necessary steps to heal and recover from a dreadful and horrible disorder caused my family so much pain. I could not reconcile my commitment to finally live a life of truth and authenticity with the alienation of so many people I loved. On paper, it made sense. As I celebrated the end of my female self inhabiting a foreign body, my family felt they had lost a son, a brother, and worst of all, a father. The cure for my disorder brought them incredible pain. Rather than trying to reconcile these impossible conflicts, I surrendered to the humbling reality that only God can understand God's plan. Human beings are not privy to the larger Divine plan. This became a much stronger test of my trust in God than grappling with my crippling disorder and my miserable and painful life until this point.

Still, my journey was nearly complete. All that was left to do on the "list" was to undergo the actual surgical procedure. By January 2005, I had chosen my surgeon and contacted her to confirm the date. Her next available date was at the end of September. I felt extra blessed, since most women who elected

Dr. Marci Bowers to perform their surgery had to fly to Denver from all over the United States. They then needed to rent a car to drive the 200 miles from the airport to the small hospital where she practiced at that time in Trinidad, Colorado. I was still living in Colorado Springs, less than a two-hour drive away.

During the summer I made all the necessary arrangements, and as the date drew closer and closer I felt increasingly excited. I was ready. It was the right time. Well, almost.

I received a call from Dr. Bowers, or Marci as her patients would call her. Marci said that she appreciated how I must be counting down the days to the day. After all, she herself had undergone the same journey a few years before me and transitioned from Dr. Mark Bowers to Dr. Marci Bowers, when she held the position of head of OB/GYN at the Swedish Medical Center in Seattle, WA.

However, she had a very special favor to ask of me. Due to a last-minute invitation to deliver an important talk at a medical convention on my originally scheduled date for the surgery, she asked if I would consent to delaying my surgery by one week, into the first week of October. Whether she would accept the invitation to speak at this medical convention or not rested entirely upon me. I told her that after waiting over fifty years to finally receive the proper body for my soul to inhabit, I could surely wait one more week. After all, what was I transitioning into if not a more kind, compassionate, and gentle person? Adding to that my belief that every detail of my life was under God's direction and personal supervision, how could I say no? Not looking at a calendar, I had no idea how fortuitous my revised date would be.

On Tuesday morning, October 4, 2005, I eagerly awoke early, double-checked my bag, and drove to Trinidad,

Colorado. Not a family member was with me. Not a friend. I drove alone, and yet, not for a second did I feel alone. I felt safe and secure, as I resided within the protective womb of my Creator. As I approached the city limits, I realized I was several hours early for my pre-op hospital check-in appointment.

I pulled to the side of the road and just stared, or rather gazed, at the beauty of the Rocky Mountains. It was a clear day, and the view was nothing less than majestic. Suddenly, I had an eerie feeling. I felt something that I had sought for years when I was Orthodox and when I lived in Jerusalem. Here I was, physically alone, approaching a tiny little town in southern Colorado in preparation for what would be my most life-changing moment since birth. I felt kedusha, holiness or sacredness, like never before. I became aware of God's presence like never before. I sensed there was an extra dose of kedusha, of awareness of God's presence beyond my own limited self and perception.

I called my mom to tell her I was about to check into the motel room I had reserved for the evening. She asked me if I had plans to attend synagogue before my surgery. I was puzzled. "Why do you ask?" I wondered aloud. She was even more puzzled than me at my response. She said, "Because it's the first day of Rosh HaShanah!"

My mother's words startled me. I was so focused on my upcoming surgery that I never bothered to look at my calendar. Now I understood what it was I was feeling as I gazed at the mountains. This was the first day of Rosh HaShanah and the final day in my life that I was forced to dwell in a foreign body. The Jewish tradition believes that Rosh HaShanah is the Day of Judgment, when God decrees for all His creations who will live for another year and who will not. I felt the decree that a part of me, a broken part of me, a hurting part of me, a dreadful part of me had been decreed to die. Nevertheless, it was a part of me, and on the first day of Rosh HaShanah I needed to grieve its death and loss. This is why I arrived early. This is why I pulled to the side of the road to gaze and reflect. This is why I called my mother. This is why Dr. Bowers asked me months ago for my consent to change the date. It was a Divine decree from above revealed in the most concrete way possible.

That evening I had dinner with a few other women who were scheduled for their surgery the next day as well. I explained to them that this was Rosh HaShanah, and we blessed each other for a healthy new year in our new bodies. I shared with them the Jewish tradition of dipping pieces of apple into honey as a symbol of our asking God to bless us with a sweet year ahead. I went to sleep feeling incredibly blessed. Blessed to be exactly at the right place at the right time doing the right thing. And blessed to feel closer to God than ever before.

The next day, the second day of Rosh HaShanah, I arose early, checked into the hospital, and was prepped by a nurse for the surgery, and as I was wheeled into the operating room I gently and quietly said good-bye to my past and hello to my future.

I woke up a few hours later in what would be my room for the next week. A nurse came in and informed me that, thank God, the surgery had been successful and without any complications.

Marci came by a few hours later to check on me. She examined me and asked how I was feeling. I looked at her, right into her eyes, and thanked her. With tears in my eyes, I blessed her for being God's angel who not only saved my life, but even more than that gave me a new one. What a precious and humbling gift my Creator gave me, employing her as His messenger, as His angel, on the second day of Rosh HaShanah. What an amazing way to begin the new year ahead—the newest new year ever.

Chapter 35

STARTING OUT FRESH

Time to move on and start out fresh. I knew that I was on my way back to Israel, but not just yet. It wasn't time. I trusted in God that when it was time to return home, I would know. In November 2005, I applied for a transfer with Starbucks, and upon approval I began my new life in Seattle. Close to the famous Pike Place Market, I managed one of the oldest and busiest stores in the company. I did not know anyone in Seattle when I moved, and yet, I intuitively sensed that this was where I was destined to be until my eventual return to Israel.

On my first Friday night in Seattle, with childlike excitement and a twinkle in both eyes, I began to observe a very special mitzvah—one of God's commandments—a time-honored tradition that I longed to keep since discovering my

Jewish identity in Israel in 1971. Shortly before sunset, I ushered in Shabbat in the traditional way that Jewish women have been doing for more than a thousand years. My maternal great-grandmother brought this tradition with her from Poland to New York in the 1880s. My maternal grandmother continued in Brooklyn, as did my mother on Long Island. And now, in Seattle, at the age of fifty-four, I felt privileged to continue this sacred tradition in my family's lineage. I lit the Shabbat candles, then waved my hands over them, covered my eyes, and for the first time in my life uttered the special blessing as I officially welcomed the arrival of Shabbat.

I gazed at the Shabbat candles as their yellow-orange glow illuminated not only my tiny one-room studio in downtown Seattle, but my inner being as well. The flames cast the most exquisite shadows against the wall. With the lighting of the Shabbat candles, I ushered a new light into my new life. I sat and reflected on the miracle inherent in this cathartic experience. All I could say was Baruch HaShem—Thank God—for the Divine kindness with which I was now blessed.

I strongly sensed a connection with Jewish women all over the world, both with those who preceded me for centuries and with all those living souls who lit this evening as well. I thought of the countless Jewish women who committed themselves to carry on the tradition, week after week, introducing new light into a dark world under circumstances I could not even imagine. In my cozy, comfortable, and safe apartment in Seattle, I imagined what it took for the Jewish women before me to do what I had just done. These women lived in Europe during the Crusades, in Spain during the Inquisition, in Russia under the sadistic Czarist rule, and then during the darkest period in Jewish history, the Holocaust. Then there were the Jewish women who kept the tradition alive in Northern Africa, in the Mediterranean countries, and in the Arab lands. And with a jolt I remembered all the thousands and thousands of Jewish women who risked their lives lighting candles in their very homeland, Israel, while under foreign occupation by hostile governments, one after the next, since the Romans destroyed the Second Holy Temple in 70 CE.

Many thousands of Jewish women had ushered in this very same Shabbat with me, one time zone after the next. Israeli women and women living on every continent in the Diaspora; Sephardic and Ashkenazic women, and those from the Arab lands east of Israel; great-grandmothers, women raising families, and young brides. I connected to my past, present, and future all at once, knowing that my mother and my own daughters and daughters-in-law lit candles that Friday night as well. I became aware at that moment that my gender transition journey now took me to a space where I touched spiritual immortality. I officially took my place in the long line of my own Jewish lineage, being the midpoint now between those women in my family who preceded me and those who followed me. In a way, this became my first real Shabbat—my very first Shabbat as my true, genuine, authentic self.

When I went to sleep on that first Friday night, I also became aware of something completely new in my life. For over fifty years I could be in a room with scores of people and feel painfully alone and lonely. Of course, I was disconnected from my own self and estranged from God. As I lay under the covers, physically alone in my room, I did not feel lonely. I felt hugged, cuddled, and protected by my Lover of lovers. As I drifted off to sleep, it was as if God whispered in my ear, "As long as you are with Me, you will never ever again be lonely. I will always be with you, no matter what. Just don't ever let go."

It was now time to find my place, my new place, within the Jewish community. As with my gender transition journey, there was no recipe, especially for a single woman who is fifty-four years old and new in town. And as with my gender transition journey, I assumed the role of the follower and not the leader. One of the many lessons I had learned the hard way was to proceed slowly and carefully. My reasons for wanting to rejoin the Jewish community were not rooted in insecurity and self-loathing but rather longing to once again be a part of the Jewish experience. Jewish people experience their souls, their heritage, and their identity both in the privacy of their home and in the public setting. Being a member of the Jewish community allows for expression in both domains. As I began to develop my own Jewish home, I likewise felt the tug to be with other like-minded souls in community.

As I began to meditate and ponder on the various synagogue communities in Seattle, I felt, in the most humble of ways, incredibly empowered.

The Jewish tradition teaches that "a little bit of physical light pushes away vast amounts of darkness." Likewise, in Proverbs 20:27, we read: "The soul of a person is the lamp of God." So now I deduced that I had within me a tiny flame, a little lamp. When I entered a dark space, by simply honoring my truth and living authentically, allowing my own spirit to surface and shine forth, I could push away huge amounts of darkness and shed light on those around me. This boggled my mind! I could actually do that? I asked myself. The part of me that is God, this little lamp, in fact could, and would! But only if I remained true to the real me.

I then realized I did not have to rush to become a member of any particular synagogue community. I could visit various congregations in Seattle, and as both an observer and a participant, experience what it would be like for the light in me to push away any darkness around me. In this way, I would be able to test the waters and gain a better sense of where in fact I most belonged and with whom I connected most strongly.

Chapter 36

RIGHTING THE PAST

Shortly after I moved to Seattle in 2006, I had my American passport, Social Security card, and driver's license officially changed to reflect my proper gender marker. In all these cases, the only proof of gender change that I was required to submit was a letter from my surgeon. Quite easy and uneventful for the clerks who pushed through my paperwork, this simple act was life changing for me. Each corrected document contributed to the healing of my soul.

I had a new identity, at long last, and now every official document in my life acknowledged that identity. All but one. Although it was not required of me to do so, I felt I needed to have a new birth certificate issued in order to right my past retroactively and not only my present and future.

Many of the women who undergo gender transition do not bother with this. But for me, correcting a document that had been issued at birth would once and for all acknowledge the truth I had lived with my whole life. I was born a woman. I had always been a woman. I wanted a piece of paper with a stamp on it to have and to hold, to prove what I had known all along to be true.

To my pleasant surprise, this was much less complicated than I had anticipated. When I called the New York State Department of Health for advice on how to proceed, the Director of Vital Records himself answered the phone. He seldom answered the phone himself, but due to a series of unusual and unexpected circumstances that particular day at that particular time, he in fact answered my call. After outlining the necessary steps I was required to follow, he assured me that the appropriate paperwork for me to complete would be sent out that day. Unsolicited, he gave me his direct line and urged me not to hesitate to use it if I encountered any questions or problems. As I hung up, I was almost in shock with joy and gratitude. So many of my fellow post-op women had relayed horror stories of obstacles and resistance, and yet, so far it had been smooth sailing for me.

The papers came quickly and were returned just as quickly, and on March 3, 2006, not even a full five months since my life-changing surgery, fifty-four years and eight months to the day after my birth, my birth certificate was officially changed. I received it a few days later. I read the words over and over again: "Jessica Sara Smith, female, born 03 July 1951 at 10:10pm in Suffolk County, Bay Shore." The local filing date read "06 July 1951." I could not restrain myself from weeping. In what seemed like a mere fleeting moment in time, the government had recognized and corrected a whole lifetime. My past was retroactively righted. All I could say as I looked up to heaven with tears of gratitude streaming down my face was Baruch HaShem, Thank God! And I said Baruch HaShem with all the intent and focus I could muster.

Of course, this one document, as significant as it was for me, was the precursor to yet another vital step on my path to healing. I needed to make things right with my mother, the woman who had given birth to the baby girl on that very birth certificate. My transition had been difficult for everyone in my family, but above all else the pain it caused my mother was the hardest for me to bear. Even more than the failure and disappointment I lived with regarding the bewilderment I had caused my precious children, the hurt my mother endured plagued me incessantly. I believed that in time my children would heal from their trauma, as I had healed, but I was not sure the same could be said for my mother.

Hurting my mother, who inherited from her mother the strongest unconditional love and loyalty any child could ever hope for, simply broke my heart. My entire life, I strove to make her feel proud of me and grateful for having conceived me, having carried me in her womb, having given birth to me, and having raised me, her first child. After all, as miserable as I felt for the first fifty years of my life, as much as I hated my life for half a century and as much as I suffered tremendously for five decades, I knew it was no one's fault. I truly believe that if my mother had known for all that time how much horrific pain I endured, she would have done everything possible to provide me the necessary healing. But she did not know. She had devoted her life to protecting and nurturing her children, and I had denied her the opportunity to help me for over fifty years. It was as if my actions belied her role in life.

In the winter of 2005, I spent weeks preparing a letter to my parents advising them of my transition and upcoming surgery in the fall. I meditated, sought God's guidance to find the right words, wrote and rewrote countless times. Over the course of several weeks, I finished the most difficult, heart-wrenching letter I ever had to write and sent it to the two people who bestowed upon me the gift of life.

I had not seen my parents since the winter of 2004, a year earlier. During that visit, when my father was alone with me, he said, "I want to ask you something, but please try not to be upset or defensive." His sentiment clearly communicated concern. He asked me if I was aware that with each visit to Florida over the past several years, I was appearing increasingly female in my demeanor and mannerisms. He also told me when he discussed this with my mother she implored him not to mention his feelings to me. She was, he said, in complete denial of the situation, and angrily asked him not to discuss this with me. He argued back that he could ask his son whatever he wanted. He was indeed correct. I replied that I was not really clear how I appeared to both him and my mom. I was aware that I was increasingly allowing myself to express my true identity, but I was not yet ready to discuss my transition with him in person. He was shocked at my relaxed tone when answering him, and told me so.

Following this honest and candid discussion, one of the few I ever recall having with my father, he informed my mother what had transpired. She became livid and actually yelled at my father in front of me for having brought this up with me. With a victorious grin on his face, he suggested she ask me the same question, but she would not. Perhaps she could not. He clearly told her, "I told you so." Nothing further was discussed of this during the rest of my visit.

At the end of my letter, I told them I would not initiate any phone calls. I would wait to hear from them, as I was sure this would shake them up considerably. I wanted to give them the time and space they would need to process this shattering news. I made sure to communicate to them that in no way were they at fault. I was born with a severe psychiatric disorder and hormonal imbalance. I now needed to do what was necessary to heal from a miserable life and achieve a healthier state of being. I emphasized that I could not imagine what they would be feeling, and that causing them such heartache saddened me greatly.

Within a few days after mailing the letter, my mother called to tell me they had received it. Her words echoed in my heart: "Jeffrey, you've done a lot over the years to challenge our compassion and support. But each time your father and I have supported you. Now you've gone too far. I don't know how I can ever understand what you are doing, never mind support you. Give me time, and please don't call me." My mother never told me not to call her.

Several months later, she called me out of the blue. She said that since I was scheduled for surgery soon, as my mother, she wanted to understand exactly what was involved in this procedure. From that point on, we resumed limited communication by phone. I always deferred to her taking the lead. After the surgery, the phone calls increased. She even sent me a Tiffany "silver coffee bean" pendant for my birthday in July 2006 to welcome me to my new life. This was meaningful since she had done the same for my sisters years earlier and for each of my daughters when they became bat mitzvah at twelve years old.

After I moved to Seattle, we spoke on the phone more frequently, and eventually Mom suggested I come visit her. In her wisdom and grace, she spared me the possible rejection that I might have faced if I had been the one to take the lead. I waited and waited and waited, and prayed and prayed and prayed, that one day during a phone call she would say that she wanted to see me. In time, she did. This was the longest period of time we had endured without seeing each other, including when I had lived in Israel for all those years.

She sadly informed me that my father would not see me on this visit. He was not ready and did not know when or if he would ever be. From the time I sent the letter until now, he spoke to me only once, the day prior to my surgery. He said he could not even speak to me about what I was about to do but he wanted me to know that he hoped I would be spared any medical complications and that I would remain healthy.

After landing at the West Palm Beach Airport, as I was driving toward her home in Delray Beach, FL, all of a sudden I realized the significance of the day. It was to be a momentous day. For the first time in her life, my mother would see her firstborn child, her son, as her daughter, as a female, as Yiscah, as Jessica. For the first time in my life, I would stand before my mother clean and honest. As if this wasn't enough of a major moment in time, this visit fell on October 5, 2006, exactly one year after my surgery. Another set of "circumstances" made this date the most opportune time for me to visit.

As I approached her gated community, my heart began to beat faster. I was so excited, so overjoyed, and so nervous! The guard at the gate called my mother to announce my arrival and then waved me in. As I drove up to the house, I uttered one more last prayer to God: "Please, God, all I want to do is give my mother joy and make her feel good that she brought me into the world." With my heart beating even quicker and my anticipation building up to a climax, I pulled into her driveway. She came out to greet me. I turned the engine off and got out of the car.

We looked at each other and hugged. As we looked into each other's eyes, we both cried. She then told me something I would never forget. "Jessica, you don't have to say a thing. I have never looked into your eyes and seen what I see now. I always knew, your entire life, that something was not right. I felt it but had no idea what it was. I have never seen what I see now. I see you happy for the first time in your life." All I could do was hug her again and tell her how much I loved her. This moment ushered in a deeper, happier, and much closer relationship than either of us ever imagined we would experience.

We spent a week together talking, crying, laughing, going to the beach, going out to eat, staying in to eat, more talking, and more crying. We even went shopping together, having fun as a mother and daughter should, with her telling me in no uncertain terms what colors, fabrics, and styles looked best on me.

However, while cause for immense celebration, I was not living in an illusion. I knew that my transition caused her much stress and sadness at times. She was not ready, nor did she know if or when she would ever be, to be honest with her friends about me. She made sure to tell me in a most heartfelt way that my transition crushed her. But still, she "got it," and reassured me that her love for me did not waver and in fact she now supported me! Seeing me finally happy brought my mother so much joy, which in turn brought me a sense of much needed relief. Our emotions fed off each other. Every night during my weeklong visit, I went to sleep knowing that after almost fifty-five years I could now be completely authentic with the most important person in my life, with the very woman who gave me life, and never have to worry again. So, this visit righted the past in the most profound and important way. Now, both the woman who birthed me, and the document testifying to it, affirmed the truth that had remained hidden for so long.

Chapter 37

TIME TO GET BACK TO WORK

I was born to teach. Getting people excited about learning is my inner calling. Teaching, being in service to others' learning journeys, gives my life meaning with each new breath. As the Talmud so vividly articulates this calling, "More than the calf wants to suckle, the cow wants to nurse" (Pesachim 112a). For the past eighteen years, since I had left the Old City in Jerusalem, I was not formally teaching Torah studies, but that did not mean I ceased teaching. Wherever I worked during those eighteen years, I naturally gravitated toward employee training and development. This movement in my career significantly increased after I transferred with Starbucks to Seattle. While still officially a store manager, I began to facilitate more and more training workshops at corporate headquarters. I began to develop relationships with partners in the training and development and global diversity departments, and shadowed several people to become more experienced. It was clear to everyone around me that I was on the path out of retail and into full-time training. With my gender transition "officially" complete, I felt unfettered and more focused and excited to nurture my teaching abilities.

At the same time, I began to slowly reenter the Jewish world and explore the many avenues of expressing my Jewish identity that even a small city like Seattle had to offer. In the back of my mind, I found myself wandering back to teaching Torah studies. "No," I told myself. "Impossible. I can't do that again." I argued with myself. Where would I even begin, after all this time? I was not even sure at that point what type of Jewish community I would feel comfortable in. I was at a vulnerable juncture in my life. How could I even think of once again retaining a position of influence and leadership in the capacity of teaching Torah?

On my Jewish journey, the journey of my spirit, I felt like a beginner. Yes, I had taught for over twenty years, but not as my true self. Now, in the body of my authentic self, I could finally express my soul genuinely. No more hiding behind masks pretending to be someone other than myself. Still, surely I could not teach Torah, at least not now. This internal debate played on and on for months.

I was moving ahead in my own career path, and yet, intuitively, deep inside, I sensed my path would not lead me to corporate headquarters. Of all the lessons I had learned on my gender transition journey, one of the most valuable was to trust myself, my intuitiveness, the Godly part within me, my essential being.

By spring 2009, God began to reveal to me once again how my intuition speaks only the truth. One morning at 5am, I began the ritual of preparing my Starbucks store for opening with another partner. As the manager, I had not only the regular front-of-the-store duties to attend to but the many back-of-the-store management ones as well. Busy, busy, busy—to put it mildly. I had done this more than a few hundred times since beginning with the company in Colorado in 2003, and yet, no matter how many times I did it, and how efficiently I had learned to work, there always seemed to be too much to do in too little time. On this particular morning, I was bordering on panic as each minute ticked by quicker and quicker, and the two of us went about our work in a robotic frenzy. As usual, I noticed that customers were already impatiently lined up outside, fifteen minutes prior to opening. This time, though, I felt unusually agitated. Almost resentful.

Starbucks had already adopted several new business strategies in response to the recent drastic economic recession to salvage its plunging revenues. These were aimed primarily at keeping their investors on Wall Street content, and they cost thousands of partners their jobs. Positions at corporate were eliminated, most of my connections now faced unemployment, and 700 stores were shut down across the country. Rumors of the company terminating tenured managers' employment to replace them with a fresh crop of newly appointed ones began to circulate. My district manager assured all twelve of us store managers that neither our stores nor our positions were in jeopardy. But hundreds of people who loyally worked for Starbucks at corporate headquarters for more than twenty years had unexpectedly and suddenly lost their jobs. We were all nervous.

By this time, I knew the track I was moving on was all but history. In a single day, it evaporated into thin air. So yes, that early spring morning, at 5am, I felt agitated and resentful. I was in front of the urns preparing the first batch of coffee to be freshly brewed and ready exactly at the moment when I would unlock the doors for the line of customers to enter. We would be able to greet them with a smile and serve them as quickly and efficiently as possible.

Suddenly I heard myself say, "This cannot continue. This will not continue. This is the last time I am opening this store. I don't know how much longer I can continue working like this in this position. All chances of moving over to corporate seem extinguished. I have been created to do much more with my life. I really long to return to teaching Torah." This was indeed a self-fulfilling prophecy, and a set of unexpected events began to unfold before my very eyes.

Shortly after this 5am revelation, I received an invitation to participate in a think-tank meeting at corporate headquarters. The president of Starbucks brought together a chosen group of both retail and corporate partners to discuss ways of providing a more effective and encouraging work environment for those partners facing an assortment of both physical and mental challenges in the workplace. Being the parent of a deaf child (now an adult with her own children) and managing a high-revenue store in downtown Seattle, combined with my own personal gender transition journey, he thought I would be qualified to suggest some concrete ideas. The meeting was both productive and emotionally moving.

At the conclusion of the meeting, the president expressed his gratitude to each of us and thanked us for our participation. We said our good-byes, and off we went. That same day, I was scheduled to facilitate a workshop for store managers with my own original content. A few partners in the training and development department who had survived the brutal separations were also invited to attend. They wanted to evaluate and critique both the content I wrote and my delivery. I arrived early in order to set up the room properly and have all necessary materials ready for distribution. But around twenty minutes before I was scheduled to start, I received an odd and eerie-sounding phone call from my district manager, the person to whom I directly reported.

"Jessica, are you all ready for the workshop?"

"Yes." I replied.

"I apologize for not being able to attend, but I have a schedule conflict."

"No worries, I understand," I said.

"Oh, by chance, are you in any rush to leave after the workshop?"

"No, why do you ask?"

"Would you please stay after you're finished? I need to discuss something with you and will be right over when it's over."

"Is everything OK?" I asked.

"Yes, OK, see you later. Good luck."

My own naïveté got the better of me, and I did not assume the worst. Still, the timing and content of the conversation did not sit well with me. And this was right before I was about to facilitate a new workshop under the scrutiny of what I hoped would be my peers at corporate headquarters. If any chance of moving my career forward still existed, much was hinging on this workshop. All I could do was push her words out of my mind and focus extra hard on the workshop and its participants.

At its conclusion, I received a round of applause with congratulations on both the writing and the facilitation of a wonderful, insightful workshop. The people from corporate were all smiles and voiced their praise. They advised that within days they would send me their critique, and they looked forward to seeing me in the near future. Everyone left, and I began to clean up. I felt grateful for how everything went, but my moment of basking in my own self-congratulatory rays was short lived.

My district manager appeared within seconds after everyone was gone. Her presence cast a dark grayish feel to what had been a bright cheery space. I sensed, I knew, that this visit was not good. In less than sixty seconds, she separated me from Starbucks, effective immediately.

I sat there in shock, began to cry, and just looked at her and said, "After five and a half years of devoted service, with a file thick with letters and cards of praise from customers and executives at corporate, how could you do this to me? I was with the president this morning, and he acknowledged how grateful he is to have me working for the company. I just successfully delivered a brand-new workshop whose content I wrote." Her reply was that this was very difficult for her but some hard decisions needed to be made. She did make sure to mention that it was apparent to everyone that my cheery upbeat personality was not as evident as it usually was. Any attempts I made to explain why, which included illegal and unethical forced overtime for which I was not compensated, were met with a cold, stern countenance that would frighten the strongest of people. I was not allowed to return to my store and was required to come to her office the next morning to sign off on the separation documents. With that, she left.

I sat there and at first was so distraught, so disappointed, so upset. And then all of a sudden I felt wonderful. Let's be honest, I heard myself saying. I don't want to work for this company anymore. Even the thought of moving over to corporate no longer captured my attention as it had for the past several years. The dangling carrot seemed to dry up.

After witnessing hundreds of loyal, high-performing partners lose their positions over the course of three Friday mornings, I seriously wondered why I would even want to put myself in such a precarious position.

I was "old school" Starbucks. As each manager in my district was separated, one by one, I realized that the company was losing its soul. And as for me, I was just beginning to reclaim my own, expressing and nurturing it more than ever before. Clearly this was Godly intervention and guidance in the most revealed of ways.

And then I heard a comforting and yet directing voice calling to me within: "OK, Yiscah, I gave you your much needed break—several years off to take care of your demons, your disorder, your issues, and your health. It's now time to get back to work!"

And so began the next step on my journey. It was time to get back to work and return to my passion, my calling, and what gave my life meaning—teaching Torah.

Chapter 38

THE VIEW FROM ABOVE

I spent the next several years visiting different synagogues. Whereas before I had limited myself to the Orthodox/Chassidic world, I was now willing to broaden my spiritual horizons, provided I remain within one strict parameter: I resolved to always be honest, with myself and with others. The days of parroting back whatever I was taught or told would remain in the Dark Ages of my past.

In order for my return to Judaism to be spiritually healthy and sustainable, I needed to be intentional and proactive in my decision-making. I committed myself to remaining open to my true feelings and trusting my intuition. While I naturally gravitated to the Orthodox world, I knew that wasn't necessarily where I belonged, at least not full-time. Freed from external pressures to conform, and equally freed from fearing peer disapproval, I sought approval only from God and from Jewish law.

I never doubted for a second that the Torah contained wisdom on how to guide an individual who suffered from gender identity disorder. But I also knew that close to 100 percent of the contemporary rabbinic world were ignorant and ill equipped to respond to those in my situation who sought answers within the tradition. In this sense, I became part of a vanguard of sorts, a trailblazer, a pioneer into foreign and new territory.

Although it saddened me, I knew I would face more challenges in the Orthodox world than in the more progressive, liberal Jewish communities. The world to which I had once belonged was insular and rigid. This had served a valuable purpose in generations past. But in a contemporary, post-Holocaust world, such rigidity was off-putting. Individuals who couldn't conform to prescribed "norms" of this society were pushed away. Where did this leave me? Uncertain, but brimming with newfound optimism, I dove into the waters of Jewish communities to see where I could flourish, illuminate, and grow the most—and where I would sense HaShem's presence.

During the five-year period from 2005 to 2010, I walked through the doors of thirteen different synagogues to attend services: four Reform, one Conservative, four Orthodox, one Jewish Renewal, one independent meditation-based, one independent partner-based cooperative, and one committed to being a gathering for Jewish growth within the matrix of halacha (traditional Jewish law) observance. To my complete surprise, I found them all to have much more in common with one another than not. The members in each of these Jewish micro-communities seemed to want to be there. The very act of being in community was an important value that held the congregation together, and each community's version of the prayer service was designed to afford the congregants the best positive communal experience possible.

Likewise, except for one, none of these prayer services emphasized the individual talking to God and being in relationship with God. God was seldom talked about. The importance of being in community, contributing in various ways to the group, and remaining loyal to the community were the prevalent values. Connecting to God remained an afterthought.

For me, though, as much as I needed to be in community, I needed to experience transcendent prayer even more. I needed the service to invite me to participate emotionally and then transport me to a spiritual realm. Parts of me connected with parts of each of these communities, but not one was a perfect fit. I knew that my gates of prayer could not be found in Seattle, but only in Jerusalem, and I longed to return one day. Still, I embraced my present, and resolved to find a place where I could experience talking with God while remaining in community, rather than in the solitude of my home.

The picking and choosing I observed among every denomination was both startling and comforting. Adhering to some laws while declaring others irrelevant was sometimes difficult for the traditional part of me, but it also helped me focus on the humanity of Judaism that spanned all boundaries and went beyond any labels. This helped me forgive myself and others, be patient, and embrace humanity with all its beautiful contradictions. My tradition surely brought me up, and not down into the dark, lonely pit of harsh judgment, criticism, and arrogance.

The first time I stepped into a Chabad-Lubavitch synagogue since leaving Jerusalem in 1991, the first time I went as Yiscah, body and soul, I had no idea what to expect. Some synagogues separate the men's and women's prayer sections by placing the mechitza, the physical divider, down the middle, front to back, with men on one side and women on the other. Others place the mechitza left to right, with the men in the front section and the women in the rear. Still others build a special balcony for the women to pray upstairs, while the men remain downstairs. At Congregation Sha'arei Tefilah, on that momentous Shabbat morning, I went upstairs to sit in a designated women's balcony for the first time in my life.

For too many years in my past, my soul endured excruciating pain, having suffered the fate of an outsider, forced to pray downstairs or on the wrong side of the mechitza. The foreign body my soul was forced to inhabit at birth dictated to the Jewish world in which section I would be required to pray. Is it any wonder I could never truly focus on calling out to God in truth? The very place I called out from was a lie! I didn't belong there. I used to glance over the mechitza or subtly peek up at the ezrat nashim—the women's balcony—with hurting eyes, the longing of a soul yearning to be where she genuinely belonged, with her fellow sisters. During those years I always felt I was in the wrong place at the right time.

Until this particular Shabbat, the many synagogues I had attended boasted the lack of a mechitza or ezrat nashim. These congregations embraced egalitarianism. Women were given the same roles as men in the prayer service. Separate seating in separate prayer spaces simply did not exist. I did not find this particularly offensive or disrespectful to tradition, as it was a sincere attempt to interpret the tradition to meet a different set of needs in a different time and place. But for me, it never felt quite right. Once again I seemed to be in the wrong place at the right time.

Now the time had arrived for me to be in the right place at the right time. Incredible! I took a siddur—prayer book—from the shelf and sat down. Effortlessly, as if I had davened with only women my entire life. I felt so normal that the moment actually lacked excitement. This, too, was miraculous! I opened the siddur and began to recite the prayers with the congregation. I was talking to God, to HaShem, in Hebrew, the language of my people, words that Jewish people have uttered all over the world for centuries. I experienced focus and intentional thinking without disruptive inner noise. No static. The transmission of HaShem's presence received and responded to. While physically being in the ezrat nashim felt ordinary, talking to HaShem without demons attempting to sabotage the moment was by all means extraordinary.

There is a line in the Shabbat service that used to make me cringe with guilt, having felt so spiritually filthy. That Shabbat morning as I said, "Purify our hearts to serve you in truth," I felt tears gently fall upon my face. I was now where I belonged. I glanced at the men and thought to myself, "The view from above, looking down, is so much better!"

Chapter 39

YOUNG LOVE

Shortly after I moved to Seattle, I dove headfirst into the pool of dating. This would be the first time that I would be looking to meet men as a full-fledged woman. Before my transition, I felt I needed a man in my life to validate my self-worth and sense of self. I sought connections with men within a personal vacuum. While my relationship with Richard afforded me genuine moments of intimacy and sharing of hearts, it was as doomed as all the others to fail.

Now, in Seattle, my experience was entirely new. For the first time, I experienced the joy of being alone, of enjoying my own company, and feeling HaShem's presence daily. My desire to date came from a healthy need for companionship. At the age of fifty-five, I did not seek out a man with whom to build a family or to complete me. Rather, I sought someone to connect with, to feel close to, and to share meaningful and not-so-meaningful times together.

In a way, I felt like a young woman learning how to navigate the waters of male/female courtship—awkward but eager. At the same time, I started developing friendships with other women, and they brought unexpected fulfillment and joy to my life. It was effortless to be with other women. We seemed to naturally understand each other. Nurturing these connections involved supporting and encouraging each other. I welcomed this new way of being with other people.

However, I felt equally drawn to men for completely different reasons. I wanted to experience the varied expressions of intimacy with someone of the opposite sex. I signed up on a few of the dating websites, wrote up a profile, and posted a few pictures. As if in some kind of time warp, I experienced all the anxiety and anticipation that a young woman, beginning her journey to love, might have felt. I had no idea how the men I would meet would react when finding out about my journey.

Over the course of many first (and last) dates, I discovered two basic reactions from men when they learned of my transition. Some men became noticeably uncomfortable immediately. While complimenting me on my appearance when we first met in person, several men would say they didn't feel comfortable with my past. They would apologize if they were hurting me but could not entertain going out again. My reply to them was simple: "If you have a problem with my past, I have a problem with your present. So, yes, you are right, this won't work. You can't do this? I can't do this either." Others, instead, became obsessed with my having undergone transition. I ceased to be a person, a human being, and surely a woman. I was clearly an oddity that they wanted to explore. This I found outright hurtful and insulting. My reply to these men was equally poignant: "If you are so taken by a sliver of my entire being, enough to be obsessed by it, I am equally pushed away by the whole of your entire being. This won't work."

After too many dates that went nowhere fast, I decided to stop. I realized that to continue this meant at best a waste of time and effort. At worst it meant an array of hurtful feelings. So, I rewrote my profile. In as few words as possible, I mentioned that I had undergone full gender transition. I clearly stated that the type of man I sought to meet would respect me for my journey but not isolate my identity to only that. In fact, I made it clear that I wanted to meet a man who sensed his life was on a spiritual journey of sorts.

Within a week I received the following response: "Any woman who looks as beautiful as you and has gone through what you have gone through to get here is someone I would like to meet. Would you like to meet for a drink?" I replied, "Thank you, and yes, I would." In September 2008, I met Dan for the first time. We easily became friends and began seeing each other frequently—but this time not to the exclusion of my friends, who at this point were mostly women. Both of us were gainfully employed, educated, well traveled, and divorced. Between the two of us, we had twelve children. I became aware that he began to enhance my happiness but that he did not define it. I embraced the sense that he increased my already existent sense of self-worth.

While fully aware of my past, Dan wanted to get to know me as a whole person, in the present. He saw me only as a complete woman and made me feel that way. I will always be grateful to him for bringing my transition to its complete state. For the next two years, we enjoyed a wonderfully fulfilling relationship. We traveled together, went hiking in the Cascade Mountains, went skiing, to the beach, to movies, to clubs, stayed in and enjoyed quiet time together and with other couples. He loved my cooking, especially those dishes from the Jewish tradition. We even took ballroom-dancing lessons together. For him, it was his first time; for me, my first as a woman. We failed miserably at it but had so much fun together trying.

He told me that no other woman, including his previous wives, had ever made him feel as happy and respected as I did. My reply back was that no man had ever made me feel so good, so valued, so loved for being the woman I naturally am. We had heartfelt discussions about family, career, my past, his past, and our present. Eventually, he moved into my apartment in downtown Seattle and we continued to strike a healthy balance between together time and alone time. At times he would go with his guy friends and I would be with my girlfriends. We lived well together, and seldom did either of us feel forced to be other than who we genuinely were. We both felt blessed and grateful. In my whole life, I had never been so happy, so full of laughter.

All my girlfriends remarked to me how he would look at me with so much love and respect. They all told me he was a "keeper."

But. Of course, there had to be a "but."

Dan was not Jewish. He grew up in a Protestant family in a very small town in Texas. In addition, he seldom thought of his life as being on a spiritual journey. As this was becoming clearer and clearer to me, I was becoming closer and closer to returning to observant Judaism. More of my life began to include observing my spiritual heritage. Eventually on Sunday mornings I began to cook two breakfasts: the traditional American bacon-and-eggs extravaganza for Dan, and my own kosher meal.

As I began exploring different Jewish community settings, he would accompany me, but I could tell this was difficult for him. I reassured him many times that I did not expect him to join me on this part of my journey. So much of my life seemed to always be dwelling in irony. Richard and I reached amazing places of spiritual depth together, but he could not accompany me on my gender transition journey, nor should he have. Dan and I, as a heterosexual couple, as two human beings, experienced so much in common, with so many layers and expressions. Yet, he could not accompany me on my Jewish spiritual journey, nor should he have.

By the fall of 2010, I sensed that this could not continue. It was not right anymore—to neither my soul nor his. I did not know how to separate from him with respect and sensitivity, in a loving way. We loved each other, and each of our hearts held a piece of the other's within us. How could I do this? I turned to HaShem and sought guidance, inspiration, and direction.

I believed with all my fiber that HaShem brought us into each other's lives for special, important reasons, which included healing. Yes, we brought each other healing, but that would begin to wither away if I continued to be with him, and I knew it. Daily I turned to God for a sign of how to proceed.

Within a short time I received the loving Divine intervention I hoped for. After work one day, Dan looked worried and concerned. He lacked his usual spunk and smile. I asked him if he was feeling OK, and he replied yes but he had something difficult to tell me. I braced myself for bad news. My thoughts turned to his health, as he had suffered a heart attack a year before we met.

With care and caution, he reminded me that he had never liked living in Seattle. Meeting me was a salvation of sorts that kept him happy in a part of the world that he did not really care for. His position with Boeing was lucrative and prestigious, but if not for that, he would not have moved to the Pacific Northwest. He likewise reminded me how much he longed to return to his home state of Texas. "OK," I replied, "and…?"

That day at work his supervisor told him that he was chosen within his division to transfer to the Austin facility in Texas to supervise the final touches on the Dreamliner airplane production. I could sense his excitement, but at the same time he made sure to temper this joy with concern. Concern for me. He invited me to move with him but knew this would be out of the question. I looked up to heaven, and then looked at him and said, with a smile of relief, "Baruch HaShem!"

We talked about our journeys going in different directions, both physically and spiritually. It was time to say good-bye. Within two months, he helped me move to the Jewish neighborhood in North Seattle, near the synagogues and Jewish community. We moved on a Sunday, and the following Friday, December 24, Christmas Eve, we hugged each other for the final time, wished each other well, and said our good-byes. We also thanked each other for being a part of each other's lives. It was a parting of dignity, love, and respect.

That first Friday in my new home, Erev Shabbat, I officially returned to observant Judaism as defined by the traditional Jewish law. As I ushered in Shabbat, with the lighting of the candles, I felt as if I had never left nineteen years earlier. Observing Shabbat and setting up a kosher kitchen came naturally—only this time I began to express my Jewish identity and soul from a place of tikkun and from a place of emet (truth).

While I continued my soul journey along the path of returning to God and Torah as a single woman, I went forth with the confidence and security of knowing I could be the woman I had always wanted to be when in a relationship with a man, thanks to Dan.

Maybe someday I will meet “a nice Jewish man” to grow old with. If God wills it, it could be wonderful and special, and if God does not will it, then my life can and hopefully will still be wonderful and special.

Chapter 40

YOU KNOW TOO MUCH FOR A WOMAN

Becoming a member in the Jewish community became increasingly important to me, especially as I sensed the Divine mandate to get back to work. As any other new arrival, I went about meeting and connecting with people in a community by volunteering. There is nothing more guaranteed to provide successful passage into a Jewish community than volunteer work.

While I began to look for work in the non-profit, social justice realm, I began to volunteer for the Jewish Federation of Greater Seattle. My extensive background in Jewish text learning combined with having made aliyah to Israel afforded me a quick entryway. I began to connect with many people within the Seattle Jewish world at large.

I also started attending a weekly Torah learning session sponsored by the Kavana Cooperative, a self-proclaimed "independent Jewish community [that strives] to create a supportive communal environment in which individuals and families can use 'kavana'—intention—to create a Jewish life that is spiritually fulfilling, intellectually satisfying, fun, and meaningful." This was a community that clearly resonated with my soul and my new way of thinking about my Jewish identity.

I longed to learn Torah again even more than to daven in communal prayer. For all those years in Manhattan, Brooklyn, Israel, Long Island, and again back in Israel, I felt like a complete fraud when davening on the men's side, the wrong side, of the mechitza. However, when I learned Jewish texts, I became so immersed in connecting to HaShem's teaching that my own gender identity dysphoria took a backseat to my intellectual pursuits.

By summer 2009, the time had arrived to return to learning Torah, in preparation for my return to teaching Torah. I had not ventured forth to a Torah learning class for over eighteen years, but now I found myself in the home of Kavana's rabbi, ready for her weekly Living Room Learning class. I walked into her home with no expectations. I was immediately drawn to sit next to a wonderful woman, Diane, who would turn out to become a dear friend of mine.

The rabbi greeted everyone and, as with each Wednesday evening class, asked each person to introduce themselves and to share with the group one thing that had happened during the course of the week that was either significant or unusual. I introduced myself and briefly said that I was exploring various Jewish communities in Seattle to see where I might fit in. Intentionally, I left out both my extensive background and experience in the traditional Jewish world as well as my gender transition journey. Just being there was profoundly significant and unusual for me.

She passed around the text we would be learning that evening and began reading. Immediately I knew I was at the right place at the right time. I had to remind myself that it had been eighteen years since I studied a Jewish text. Suddenly, as if the gates of a long-lost memory were opened wide, my mind became flooded with insights, memories, and ideas that were over eighteen years old. I spontaneously engaged in the lively discussion that began. To my further surprise, I actually began to cry. Now that was an odd sight to behold!

Until that moment I had not a clue as to how parched with thirst I was, how ravenously hungry, to eat and drink my tradition's spiritual teachings again. No one could have prepared me for this epiphany. While finding the right place to talk to God was rather difficult, finding the right place to listen to God could not have been easier, nor more exhilarating. I had no idea what "movement" within Judaism I would gravitate toward. But it was clear, absolutely clear, that I needed to reengage with the wonders of Torah learning.

Over snacks after class, more than a few of the participants approached me, introduced themselves, and expressed how wonderful it was to have met me, with the hope that I would return. And return I did. Every Wednesday evening for the next half year. That night I returned home celebrating my Judaism while honoring my inner truth within my reclaimed Jewish identity.

As the weeks turned into months, I found myself more and more involved both at the Jewish Federation and at the Kavana Cooperative. I felt the pull to return to a more traditional approach but yet felt no rush. I kept telling myself, as I did through my transition, "one day at a time." This was yet another transition for me. The many lessons I learned from my previous transition I now applied to my current one. I kept sensing healing and redemption on my journey. Each day, the simple act of being "real" brought with it miraculous, unexpected sensations of healing and redemption. Some may say these were miracles. Yes, I beheld God's presence now in the most loving and intimate ways, ways that evaded me for almost twenty years. Of course, this was a miracle. It defied the norm of what "should" have happened in my life. No one but God Himself could have predicted this. I was being given a second chance, and this time I would value it for the preciousness that it contained, whose value was beyond measure.

By the winter, my inner calling to teach took on a more definitive expression. The rabbi was going on maternity leave for three months. This meant no Living Room Learning for a while, unless various partners volunteered to either host or teach until she returned. An appeal went out for both. I took a deep breath, meditated, and realized this was the sign. Not too long before this, I felt God clearly messaged to me what I needed to do. Now, through circumstances that seemed to occur independently of my own journey, God let me know it was time! So, I volunteered to teach one of the Wednesday evening Living Room Learning classes.

Once again I was at the right place at the right time, and I sensed it. Enthusiastically, I went about preparing for the class. Immersed in my research, I was the real, authentic me, Yiscah. This realization sent shivers of gratitude down my back. For so many years, I taught as someone others wanted and expected me to be. I loved to teach and to help facilitate the spiritual journeys of others, but in the past I was a fraud, teaching what I would refer to as the truth. Now, I was true to myself, teaching what each person would interpret as being true for him- or herself. What a contrast!

It was "like riding a bike," as they say. I got right back on and pedaled away. My students were engaged, they felt safe to ask about whatever was challenging them, and I was more excited to be sharing this moment with everyone than I ever remembered in my teaching career. I also felt privileged for the first time. Several of the partners asked when I would teach again. Others asked if I would teach my own class on Jewish spirituality and mysticism after the rabbi returned from her maternity leave. I was off and running, and soon began to fly with a newly discovered exuberance and wings that felt free to spread out as far as they could.

I began teaching a class at Kavana weekly after the rabbi returned. This position led to several more, and my teaching career began to be reestablished. I began substituting in the adult education program of a local Conservative synagogue, and soon I was teaching three of my own classes there.

The teacher for whom I had originally substituted at the synagogue approached me at services one Shabbat morning shortly before the start of the academic year in 2010. We immediately struck up a lively and dynamic conversation around how each of us understood our role as a Torah teacher. Then, seemingly out of nowhere, she said, "Yiscah, how would you like to teach at the local Jewish day school?" I had never taught in an elementary school, so I immediately backed away from the idea. She urged me to consider it, and after Shabbat put me in touch with the head of the school. Within a week, I interviewed, was given an offer, and a week later began teaching fourth-grade Judaic studies at the Seattle Jewish Community School.

Within a year, I was once again passionate about my job. Not for a second did I miss working in the retail business environment. I often thought to write my prior district manager a thank-you note for separating me on that June day in 2009.

As I returned to teaching Torah with commitment, focus, and gratitude, I felt increasingly drawn to returning to a more traditional way of Jewish spiritual living as well. I began attending a weekly Torah class given by a Chabad-Lubavitch woman living in my new neighborhood. As with Kavana's Living Room Learning and with my own class, which by now had evolved into my own private independent venture, the class was hosted in someone's home.

I was thrilled to again be learning with more Hebrew texts, and yet, I felt a good bit of internal tension. This style of learning was all too familiar and quickly brought me back to a difficult time and place in my past. With my new perspective on life, and with my years of experience, I noticed for the first time a certain lack of critical thinking on the part of these participants. While I loved learning with fellow women, the class lacked a certain vibrancy, a luster, an excitement that I now knew was essential for me to thrive and grow.

My involvement with this Orthodox Jewish women's group was short lived, for many reasons. I had been received very well, and many of the women looked forward to my participation. It was apparent to them that I brought to the class a wealth of experience and exposure to classic Torah text and some of the varied rabbinic commentaries. As well, I displayed an eagerness to learn from the others that everyone equally appreciated.

One evening I arrived a bit early and offered to help the hostess set up the refreshments. I felt uncomfortable with some of the questions that she innocently asked me out of curiosity. In the Jewish world, this is referred to as "Jewish geography," and it really is amazing how within a few minutes, people who barely know each other find common connections. But in my case, this was not so simple, so I decided to just do what I was committed to doing. Without missing a beat, I told her the truth about my past. At first, she retained her composure. Then her complete discomfort with my past became apparent. In fact, she made it perfectly clear just how uncomfortable she indeed felt.

I stayed for the class that evening and even came to a few more before I realized I was no longer welcome. Invitations to come for Shabbat dinner, which were so plentiful at first, ceased from most of the women. What I shared with the hostess became news for public consumption. That in itself did not bother me, since I felt no reason to keep my past a secret, especially since my gender transition journey itself had brought me back to Torah and living a spiritual life as defined by the Jewish tradition. However, I had no reason to constantly chatter with others about my past. I much preferred to live in the present. Of course, when asked, I freely shared my experiences. What bothered me was how these women stopped identifying me as Yiscah. I became an oddity that they could not "figure out," an oddity who, in their opinion, had chosen a life that contradicted the Torah. To many of these women, my present ceased to exist and they became obsessed with my past. I knew I could not continue allowing my soul to be in such a dark place characterized by closed-mindedness, ignorance, and fear.

As if the general atmosphere were not enough, one remark in particular pushed me out the door, never to return. It spoke volumes of a world I did not want to reenter. The hostess told me that now that she knew about my past, her intuition about me made sense. Before she elaborated, I was all set to hear the typical remarks that people make toward transitioned women when realizing the "truth" about our past (as if we are the only ones with a past). Your height, your voice, your body shape, your "this" and your "that" messaged something of a male background. Instead, she said, "Yiscah, I could sense something was different about you, as you clearly know too much for a woman."

That did it. I was in no way about to "dumb down" in order to be accepted. God blessed me with a mind that I intended to use to honor, glorify, and serve Him. So, in the spirit of living an authentic life, I was denied any opportunity to teach in this Orthodox segment of the Jewish population, and I ceased attending the women's learning and social gatherings. Those friends of mine in the Orthodox world asked me if I was hurt or angry by this rejection. I was not hurt. I was disappointed. I could have been used as a valuable resource within the Chabad-Lubavitch community. I had so much to offer. What a shame I was not given the opportunity to share with these women all the knowledge that is typically reserved for the men in their world. Things would remain unchanged for them. As for me, it was time to move along once more.

By now, I felt the inner call to return home to Israel. It was time.

Chapter 41

THE RIGHT SIDE OF THE MECHITZA

On June 22, 2011, I found myself en route back to Israel, like an innocent woman who had just been released from jail, feeling the justice and exhilaration and residual weight of having been imprisoned for a crime I had never committed. For most of my life, I had been trapped in the solitary confinement of the wrong body. Now I was free, and I was finally heading home to the right place, at the right time, in the right body.

Six years earlier, my cell door had been unlocked. For the next six years, I'd been slowly walking toward freedom, through one door after the next. I learned to walk and talk and act like a person who was free, and my soul experienced a kind of spiritual rebirth. When I boarded the flight to Tel Aviv, I imagined myself walking the last few feet that separated my imprisoned self from the freedom of the outside world. The moment when the flight attendant opened the airplane door at Ben Gurion Airport, as I deplaned, I experienced redemption beyond my wildest dreams. No longer held captive by my inner demons in a prison of lies and deception, I breathed my first breaths back home in the Land of Israel as a freed woman. The thick, humid summer air embraced me as a loved one who had been waiting for me, waiting impatiently for the final door to freedom to be flung open.

Tears of gratitude and joy, bordering on disbelief, began to moisten my face.

I arrived in Israel for the first time as Yiscah Sara forty years to the day since my feet first touched the Holy Land in 1971. Forty complete years led up to this miraculous moment. That first summer in 1971, I celebrated my twentieth birthday in Israel, and now I was poised to celebrate my sixtieth. The years had been full and complex, to say the least. And here I was, back at home, feeling lighter than ever before.

That day I became keenly aware that I walked on the very same land that Joshua did when he led the Children of Israel into the Promised Land after their forty-year journey in the desert wilderness. I cannot imagine what my ancestors experienced 3,400 years ago as they began to walk on land that was theirs, no longer strangers in a strange land. But what I experienced that day may have been somewhat reminiscent. I entered the land that God, the Creator of all land, defined for me as my home, after my own forty-year journey, no longer a stranger in a strange land. As the Children of Israel began to breathe the air in Israel as a redeemed people, so did I.

I felt HaShem effortlessly whisk me from the plane onto the skywalk, into the terminal and through passport control, toward the baggage carousel, and then without delay through customs into the arrivals reception area. Anyone who has traveled to Israel knows that this seemingly simple process is often not so seamless. My memory is not of proactively going through these motions, but rather that God Himself "bore me on eagle's wings and brought me to Himself" (Exodus 19:4).

Two friends met me at the airport and brought me to Jerusalem. On the way, I kept repeating to myself out loud, "Baruch HaShem, thank God!" After all the many comings and goings, back and forth to Israel, my inner compass never ceased pointing "due Jerusalem." I dropped off my luggage and knew where I must go next.

It was time. I spent forty years journeying through my emotional and spiritual wilderness in order to get to this day. It was time to return to where the journey began, only this time I was noticeably different, inside and out. The one harmonious and authentic me entered the Old City through the Jaffa Gate. I walked through the Jewish Quarter, where I had lived with my family for so many years, to the overlook where I again beheld the Mount of Olives. I then descended those very same steps to the Kotel plaza—just as I had done forty years ago and countless times since then.

Only now, everything was different. I looked at everything around me for the first time with a new vision. I beheld what had evaded me for most of my life. I beheld God's presence in a way that allowed me to approach His Wall in truth, in purity. The past forty years crystallized in that one second, in that moment, when I could miraculously approach this sacred space cleansed and healed.

It took me forty years to move just a few inches from one side of the mechitza to the other.

At the moment when my feet touched the women's space for the first time in my life, nothing I had ever done until that moment felt as natural and right. It was as if everything that preceded this moment became my own personal prologue, leading me to this redemptive, almost surreal experience. This moment was pure essence, pure truth, pure goodness—pure reality. In the most eerie of ways possible, I heard a faint voice, perhaps from within or perhaps gently whispering from above, say, "Welcome home, Yiscah. Welcome to the right side of the mechitza."

With intention and focus, I walked slowly toward the Wall. I felt the same familiar, undeniable pull to touch the stones that I had experienced a lifetime ago on my first visit, and every time since. As I approached closer and closer, I felt the Shechinah—the female aspect of the Divine Presence—welcome me with open arms. She hugged me with her infinite love and compassion.

As I touched the stones and buried my face in their crevices, I dwelt in the paradox of kedusha—sacredness. At the very same moment that I ceased to feel my ego as I immersed myself into this oceanic space of the Divine, I also became aware of it. I then thanked God for returning me home, only this time healed. What I felt at that moment was what I had hoped for, yearned for, and prayed for every single time I approached the Kotel since 1971. As shivers ran through my body, as the tears fell, and as I uttered words of gratitude and praise, I knew in the deepest recesses of my very being, in the marrow of my existence, that my transition was God's loving and compassionate expression of bringing me back home—to Him, to myself, and to my spiritual center. This all culminated on that very day, in that very space at the Kotel.

From where I had always belonged, and from where I now stood, I replied to the Shechinah's welcome, "Shalom."

Chapter 42

THERE'S NO PLACE LIKE HOME, AGAIN

A brief and temporary stay, my time in Israel during the summer of 2011 would set the course for the rest of my life. Although I had to return to Seattle for the academic year, I knew that ultimately I would settle back home in Jerusalem, and I took this time to reacquaint myself with my city.

Reconnecting with my past, I also discovered newness in my present time and space. I walked the streets of Jerusalem a great deal and reflected even more. Here I was, back home—walking on the same streets where I had experienced tidal waves of harsh inner turmoil, constantly plagued by guilt. Now I experienced sweet inner joy seasoned with gratitude. In my former life, the simple act of walking the streets of Jerusalem caused acute stomach pain and anxiety. Now I walked pain free, able to breathe comfortably and think openly. No knots! No guilt! Deep sadness for the shattering my healing caused my family, but no guilt. Smiles and gratitude replaced those stomach pains from years past. I sat with self-respect and dignity, and even with a sense of wonder, in the synagogues I attended on Shabbat. Small and intimate, encouraging the worshiper to do exactly that, worship our Creator, privately be in conversation with the Almighty, through the spoken word, song, and dance while remaining in community. Without a contrived moment, these experiences lent themselves to spontaneous transcendence. I had searched for moments like these for forty years, both in Israel and abroad. I shared sacred moments in time with my fellow sisters, ranging the expanse of four generations, from newborns through women in their eighties. I felt clean and alert, anticipating the unexpected with wonder. On each Shabbat, I acknowledged the miracle my transition brought into my life—the miracle of returning home, healthy and of sound mind and spirit.

Indeed, my very existence gives testimony to the reality of the modern-day miracle. My life was no less miraculous than those that transcended the laws of nature during biblical times. Even the splitting of the Sea of Reeds and the manna descending from heaven could not exceed the depth and profundity of my own miracles. From my experience, my very life was a phenomenon that transcended the natural order of things as well. This in fact succinctly describes what being "back home" meant—dwelling in the sacred space of miracle and wonder.

This summer provided the rich and fertile spiritual soil necessary to fulfill a goal taught by one of my greatest sources of inspiration, Abraham Joshua Heschel: "Our goal should be to live life in radical amazement. Get up in the morning and look at the world in a way that takes nothing for granted.

Everything is phenomenal; everything is incredible; never treat life casually. To be spiritual is to be amazed." I began to greet each morning in radical amazement as I would say "modah ahni" using the feminine pronoun, thanking God for believing in me enough to bless me with another day where nothing is taken for granted and everything is incredible. In a few months, I had built myself a foundation, strong and stable, to stand upon as I continue my soul journey.

I began to prepare for my eventual, long-term return home to Israel. Within two weeks, I succeeded in changing my Israeli identity card, my teudat zehut, and my Israeli passport. A wonderful woman at the Ministry of the Interior graciously and warmly assisted me in the process. Each time we met, she would look at my prior teudat zehut and passport and would always echo the same question: "But who is this man in these pictures? You are such a beautiful woman, but I don't understand who this man is!" I would reply with a big smile, thanking her for the compliment in one breath, and in the next I would say, "At times I wonder myself who that is." And we would both smile at each other.

As one of my teachers, Avivah Zornberg, said, in referencing the utter joy the Children of Israel experienced when receiving the Torah at Mount Sinai, "The sheer pleasure gives birth to a 'me' that is unrecognizable." In a sense, the sheer pleasure of living with God in truth sometimes leaves me feeling that I don't recognize myself. At times, it's the "me" in the past, and at other times, it's the "me" in the present. But it's the sheer pleasure of being real, and being receptive to God's company, presence, and guidance in my life, that ultimately renders my own life unrecognizable at times.

As one who had been sensing so much movement in her soul journey, that summer I gained the spiritual discipline to embrace the fact that we never really know what the next step will be. Over the past ten years, I began to put my trust in HaShem more and more. For my journey to be as He intended it to be, for it to be optimal, to be maximized, and to be sensed in the deepest recesses of my consciousness as right, I needed to trust more. I began to understand that each day I must relinquish and surrender the false illusion of control that I held on to out of desperation and fear for most of my life. This in fact became the entryway to experience and even enhancing my purpose in living.

Back home in Israel, I felt compelled to surrender, but with trust, to strive to be tamim, whole, to immerse myself in the present moment without distraction, and with kavana, intentional thinking, all leading to intentional living. I found myself on the cusp of realizing that this in fact is the essential ingredient to guiding a person on one's soul journey. If it takes forty years of wandering in one's own spiritual, mental, and emotional wilderness for this mind-set to surface, then all the wandering leads to spectacular wonder. Clearly, my countless journeys back and forth were not in vain. This wandering-leading-to-wonder produced a cathartic journey—unexpected, unimaginable, and not contrived.

By the end of the summer, I found myself once again at Ben Gurion Airport, this time at the departures lounge. I had just come from an emotional farewell at the Kotel, and even the duty-free shop brought tears to my eyes.

I felt as if my insides were being torn out. For forty years I journeyed, and journeyed, and journeyed, wandering to and from Jerusalem, back and forth. Each time different and unique, each time bringing me closer and closer to truth, to tikkun, to HaShem, and to the Godly aspect immanent within me. On my sixtieth birthday, back at the Kotel after seven years of separation, I finally felt truly at home, basking in a cocoon of spiritual enlightenment, healing, wholeness, and awareness I never dreamt could be possible in my lifetime.

And now I had to leave, to tear myself away from such splendor and beauty. I knew it would be temporary, but it pained me nonetheless.

As if God Himself was speaking to me at the airport, I heard Him say, "Yiscahleh, take a deep breath from within you, open your heart and take that deep breath, and trust in Me. Return to Seattle and connect, in as authentic, genuine, and loving a way as possible, and I will return you home. But you first need to connect to a deeper place within yourself in order to help others connect to their spiritual essence, to their souls, in any way you can." As if HaShem was both commanding me and embodying me within His special mission, I felt the immediacy and humbling privilege of receiving such a command and being capable of undertaking such a holy endeavor. I felt able to bear the pain of separation for the sake of this highest calling. I knew I would be taking a piece of Jerusalem back with me to Seattle. It was now permanently embedded and engraved in my soul.

As I took my final step, lifting my foot off the Holy Land of Israel and putting it down on the floor of the plane, I kept repeating, "Thank You, God, for allowing me to return home!"

EPILOGUE

WHAT IS, IS, AND WHAT ISN'T, ISN'T

With immense gratitude to God, I moved back home to Israel in the summer of 2013. Today I live in the Nachlaot neighborhood of Jerusalem. After my forty-year journey in the wilderness, after traveling on such an extraordinary path, I find myself living a blissfully ordinary life. Not ordinary in the sense that it lacks vibrancy and dynamism, but ordinary in the sense that now I am home—with myself, with God, with others, and in Israel. Personal anguish, and the denial of it, no longer defines my life. I no longer focus on the exhausting and futile attempt to transform self-delusion into reality. My life has now blossomed into one dedicated to authentic, truthful, and genuine living.

In the late 1980s, I had the opportunity to witness the sunrise from atop Masada, an ancient Herodian fortress overlooking the Dead Sea. I sat by myself, writing in my journal while gazing at the huge orange-yellow ball gracefully rising out of the water. The Dead Sea, far from lifeless at that moment, birthed a new day for all of creation. The new rays of the day illuminated the infinite shades of browns that singularly colored the stark desert like a stage upon which the sun made its grand entry. Beholding this rare moment captivated all my attention.

Suddenly, I became aware of one of my biggest fears. The only noise I heard was my pen moving along the page, recording whatever I felt moved to write at that moment. Immediately I stopped writing, allowing myself to enter a space of sheer utter quietude. Until now, I had avoided at all costs the quieting down of my mind. Silence petrified me. Distractions, both inner and outer, numbed me from ever having to bear the truth inherent in silence. But that morning, something compelled me to enter that space of stillness. To my amazement, what I heard in that fortuitous moment was the sound of redemption, hope, and encouragement.

Since that day, I had hoped to once again hear this melody. It was a fleeting moment in my life, but I held on to it for decades. Now that I have returned home, without all the inner, out-of-tune sounds clashing with one another in my soul, I can hear this melody once again. I recognize it immediately and welcome its return. I no longer fear dwelling in harmonious quietude.

Of course, my new life here in Jerusalem is not all glorious sunrises and peaceful stillness. There are still challenges to be met, relationships that are far from perfect. One woman I had befriended soon after my move felt compelled to send me a hurtful, mean-spirited text message in the hours after the conclusion of Yom Kippur. She said she had "found out the truth" about me, as if my journey has been a safely guarded secret. Her tone was judgmental, to say the least. In my reply back to her, I invited her to meet in person, as I would not discuss this via text messaging. I politely informed her that what she had discovered was the lie I used to live rather than the truth. At that moment, I felt so much compassion for her. Clearly, her own inner demons kept her from achieving self-control and dignity, even on the heels of such a sacred holiday. She never accepted my offer to meet, nor have we seen each other since. Still, for me, it was a true moment of redemption, in which I realized that I have miraculously been freed from the powerful clutches of two demons: my gender identity disorder and my former tendency to bow to peer and community pressures.

Until my transition, my gender identity disorder consumed most of my energy, my creative spirit, and my very life. My potential to be a more loving and compassionate person never stood a chance to develop. As a result, I lived a self-centered and survival-based life characterized by fear, low self-esteem, and mistrust of others. At the same time, I lived with the false illusion that in order to fully express my Jewish identity, I needed to pledge my allegiance to one of the many movements invented by the Jewish people over the past few centuries. This tendency decried creative thinking, love of one's fellow (Jew and Gentile), and honoring the individuality of one's unique spirit. My willingness to conform was based in fear and rooted in insecurity. I was desperate to be included, and this desperation dominated much of the way I chose to live a Jewish life, and eventually drove me away from the Jewish world for many years.

It's very different now, radically different. I no longer subscribe to being a member of any movement. My community is the Jewish people at large, Klal Yisrael. How I outwardly live as a Jew is directed by the all-encompassing Jewish law—the halacha—continuously evolving in an unbroken chain from one generation to the next, in one form or another, for the past 3,400 years. This has weathered the test of time and is by far much more inclusive and comprehensive than any of the recent, limiting ideological movements that separate people from one another rather than connecting them.

In 2006, shortly before his death, Rabbi Eliezer Waldenberg, a leading Jerusalem rabbi and judge on the Supreme Rabbinical Court, ruled that male-to-female gender reassignment surgery rendered the patient halachically, officially, the new gender, that is to say, female. While this ruling is not accepted by all Orthodox rabbis (very few rulings are), it has had a tremendous impact on my own life. It further validates the fact that I am now a Jewish woman, not only in my own heart, but in the eyes of God and of government and of Jewish law. This is the real "truth about me."

When I reflect on the important classic Jewish teachings not to judge others unfavorably, I wonder where the backlash of hurtful behavior stems from. Rabbinic literature cautions us not to behave toward others in a mean-spirited, self-righteous, and intolerant way. It's painful to see how easily we can reduce ourselves to living a reactive life based on survival, rather than to be open, to truly be lights to one another and to receive one another's light.

Within the Jewish world, I strive to behave the same way with everyone I encounter. Not everyone behaves the same toward me. The judgments, the harsh snap judgments, are hurtful. But now I can honestly say that I ache more, out of compassion, for the ones who do the hurting, rather than for myself. Those who judge do so from a broken, insecure place within themselves, from ignorance, and from fear. These forces push countless Jewish people away from Judaism. These same forces, expressed in hatred, bigotry, and discrimination, prevent any human being from feeling included, desired, and valued in society.

As a child, I would look into the mirror, and what I would see looking back at me was not the truth, but rather a lie. That was in part how I experienced my inner disorder. But there is another type of a mirror, and this mirror reveals only the truth and never lies. Each of us becomes a mirror for one another, a reflection of truth. Some of us welcome what we see in this mirror of truth. We feel encouraged, safe, and affirmed, and we are filled with joy and gratitude for being honest with ourselves. Others dread the experience and run away. These people feel that their very survival is threatened and endangered.

Those who look at me and see truths of which they are afraid, truths they prefer to deny, tend to feel threatened by me, and to judge me harshly. When one lies to oneself, as I did for most of my life, one becomes estranged from who one really is. Can you imagine what it is like to be a stranger to oneself? These individuals are terrified of themselves, since they don't know themselves. They are uncomfortable with me, and with others who dare to live a life of integrity and authenticity. How could I feel anything but compassion for those people?

Of course, as a social being, I still want to be accepted by others. But now, first and foremost, I seek acceptance from God. No religion, no government, no culture, and surely no spiritual discipline can own another person's soul. Hence, I no longer seek permission or approval from others to live a life of truth. Rather, I dedicate my life, and my efforts, to being in an honest relationship with my Creator, and by extension with His beautiful world. With every inhalation of fresh breath, the Almighty Himself grants me permission to continue a life of being in service to Him.

Each one of us has our personal experience. That experience is real, and with all its joys and hurts it belongs to us, and no one can take it away from us. In part, it profoundly defines each one of us. However, each individual experience is but a piece, a very small sliver, of the big pie known as humanity.

My own transition taught me that healing one's brokenness means developing a different way of interacting with oneself and with the world. My gender transition empowered me to transition from a defensive, reactive posture to a more proactive way of thinking, speaking, and behaving, flavored with gentleness, kindness, and compassion.

I spent most of my life desperately hoping that I would someday wake up from the nightmare of my life. From a life where "what is, isn't, and what isn't, is." Now, I continuously hope to never wake up from the dream of my life. Mine is a life in which "what is, is, and what isn't, isn't." Baruch HaShem.

SOURCES OF INSPIRATION FOR LIVING A LIFE OF AUTHENTICITY

"...and then the day came when the risk to remain tight in a bud was more painful than the risk it took to blossom."

—Anaïs Nin

"A palliative nurse recorded the most common regrets of the dying. 'This is number one: I wish I'd had the courage to live a life true to myself, not the life others expected of me. This was the most common regret of all. When people realize that their life is almost over and look back clearly on it, it is easy to see how many dreams have gone unfulfilled. Most people had not honored even a half of their dreams and had to die knowing that it was due to choices they had made, or not made. Health brings a freedom very few realize.'"

—from *The Top Five Regrets of the Dying: A Life Transformed by the Dearly Departing* by Bonnie Ware

"Cézanne attacked the artificial and sentimental art of the 19th century, and showed that art must deal with the honest realities of life, and that beauty has more to do with integrity than with prettiness...When men at last accept the fact that they cannot successfully lie to themselves, and at least learn to take themselves seriously, they discover previously unknown and often remarkable recuperative powers within themselves."

—from *Man's Search for Himself* by Rollo May

"In the context of personal liberation, the final stage represents complete redemption; arriving at the place where you realize that even the pain and the suffering you experienced were actually 'good.' Though it really is hard to achieve this level and we seldom do, we do have 'small' and 'large' life examples to help us conceive and understand it. When serious medical intervention is needed to save lives, even though the intervention itself can be very painful, it is nevertheless good because a life is being saved. Until the healing is completed, the pain is still quite dominant and it is difficult to appreciate the good, but once health is fully regained, the painful process can be appreciated as having been 'good.'"

—Rabbi Sholom Brodt, Yeshivat Simchat Shlomo, Jerusalem

"Four scenes, four disguises, four failures to see behind the mask. What do they have in common? Something very striking indeed. It is only by not being recognized that Jacob, Leah, Tamar, and Joseph can be recognized, in the sense of attended, taken seriously, heeded. Do the disguises work? In the short term, yes; but in the long term, not necessarily. What we achieve in disguise is never the love we sought.

"But something else happens. Jacob, Leah, Tamar, and Joseph discover that, though they may never win the affection of those from whom they seek it, God is with them; and that, ultimately, is enough. A disguise is an act of hiding—from others, and perhaps from oneself. From God, however, we cannot, nor do we need to, hide. He hears our cry. He answers our unspoken prayer. He heeds the unheeded and brings them comfort. In the aftermath of the four episodes, there is no healing of relationship but there is a mending of identity. That is what makes them, not secular narratives, but deeply religious chronicles of psychological growth and maturation. What they tell us is simple and profound: Those who stand before God need no disguises to achieve self-worth when standing before mankind."

—from *Disguise* by Rabbi Jonathan Sacks

"There are many kinds of barriers: Those from within and those from without. Barriers between people. Barriers that prevent you from doing good things. Barriers of your own mind and your own hesitations. There are the barriers that exist simply because you are a limited being. Joy breaks through all barriers."

—from the wisdom of Rabbi Menachem Mendel Schneerson, the Lubavitcher Rebbe

"The first thing you must know before anything else applies: truth demands chutzpah—audacity. If what you are doing is the right thing to do, there will be others who will ridicule, taunt, and attempt in every way to intimidate you. That is the way the world works. If you can't handle it, if you can't ignore them as you would ignore flies on a camping trip, don't imagine you can take a single step forward. Only once you've passed the chutzpah test, only then you can begin to grow."

—attributed to the Lubavitcher Rebbe

INDIVIDUALISM

1 - The preliminary for all soul healing solutions is to take responsibility for yourself to find your own personalized solution.

2 - Outside sources and directives, even from superiors, are insufficient, and can only be a guideline—you must devise original plans for yourself.

3 - Don't stray from the advice of our holy sages of all generations, but within it, you must carve your own way, personalizing their advice as it applies to your own life.

4 - Public opinion is like a torrent river sweeping up everything in its path (including the individual mind into being brainwashed).

5 - Don't be concerned too much with what people say, and to not get swept away, you must actively swim against the current, struggling for authentic, individual, unaffected spiritual growth.

6 - A person should individuate themself with the essence of who they really are—free of social rules, cultural customs, or accepted norms—all with a mind of their own. This means bringing out that which is unique in you—so when someone will quote you—they'll say—"now that's his/her unique way..."

7 - Individuation is the key to truly exercising your free will and ultimately to reach God.

—from *To Heal the Soul* by Rabbi Kalonymus Kalman Shapira, the "Warsaw Ghetto Rebbe," the "Piaseczna Rebbe"

"Fear of HaShem is a critical aspect of liberation. Fear of man is very disruptive and causes illogical thinking. An enslaved person who is constantly being ordered about, whipped and driven with fear, is generally incapable of making good decisions. Fear of another human being brings about panic. However, fear of HaShem allows for Yishuv Ha'daat—a settled and balanced mind—the ability to make the right decisions."

—Rabbi Mordechai Yosef Leiner, the Ishbitzer Rebbe

"When we have a real spiritual stirring of the heart, or a novel and sublime idea is awoken within us, it is like the voice of an angel knocking on our door, pleading with us to let it enter our consciousness. And to the extent to which we respond with a free spirit, a pure heart, and a sincere inner yearning for Divine Love, so will there descend upon us myriad sublime souls to illuminate the darkness of our life."

—Rabbi Abraham Isaac HaCohen Kook

"Just as we accept that our neighbor's face does not resemble ours, so we must accept that our neighbor's views do not resemble ours."

—Rabbi Menachem Mendel of Kotzk

"Everybody has something wrong with them. The secret of life is to know what is wrong with me and not to cover up. One thing must be clear—if nothing is wrong with me, I wouldn't be born. I'm here to fix something. Until I am completely aware of what's wrong with me, I'm wasting my time. It is possible to know what's wrong with me and still not do it, but this is already okay. At least then—I'm already on the way.

"We all know, deep, deep down in the depth of our neshamas—souls—that there is something wrong with me and I'm afraid to tell anybody. We are always living in a certain fear. What are we afraid of? We are afraid that maybe someone will really discover what is wrong with us. I can't tell my best friend because to have a good friend to be on that level that I should tell them what's wrong with me and not be afraid that this person will stop being my friend is maybe like the friendship between David and Jonathan, which was the highest in the world.

"Reb Elimelech says a friend is somebody who you can tell what is really wrong with you and they still love you the most, and even more so. What could be is that we are even afraid to find out if we have such a friend, so we hide."

—Rabbi Shlomo Carlebach

"Imagine you're walking down the street and someone is coming toward you. Are you ready for God to be with you when you say good morning to this person? Are you ready to see with 'good eyes,' eyes through which the light of your soul is shining? 'Good eyes' are eyes that don't cut down another person, eyes that help another person see their potential and allow them and encourage them to grow."

—Rabbi Shlomo Carlebach

"There are two aspects to attaining true freedom. First, one needs to be physically independent of all foreign subjugation, freedom from any form of servitude that subjugates the divine image in man, freedom from any power that demeans the value of a human, the glory, and the holiness of man. But complete freedom also requires freedom of the spirit. The soul is not free if it is subjected to external demands that prevent it from following the path of its inner truth. What makes us truly free? When we are able to be faithful to our inner self, to the truth of our Divine image — then we can live a fulfilled life, a life focused on our soul's inner goals. One whose spirit is servile, on the other hand, will never experience this sense of self-fulfillment. His happiness will always depend upon the approval of others who dominate over him, whether this control is de jure or de facto."

—Rabbi Abraham Isaac HaCohen Kook

"And purify our hearts to serve You in truth."

—Shabbat prayer

ACKNOWLEDGMENTS

From the deepest place in my heart I express my gratitude to the following amazing holy souls, my special friends:

To Diane Hostetler for your persistent urging and convincing arguments about how important it was for me to write and publish this memoir, and for your valuable insights as I began my writing.

To Nili Ben-Ami, Tova Goldfine, Avi and Yocheved Leeker, Malika Levi Beruiti, Paul Schwartz, Aliza Weisz and Danielle Yancey for your above and beyond generous and abundant support and for your open loving-heartedness to listen to my sharing of chapters.

To Nance Adler, Deb Arnold, Andrew Cohen, Tracey Flum, Bima Goldshmid, Cherie Hershman, Stacy Lawson, Sara Morrow, James Packman, and Sharon Perlin. Each of you in your own special and loving way has supported and encouraged me significantly.

To my awesome steering committee, without whom this would not have come to fruition: Elisa Bronstein, Public Relations and Social Media Manager; Julia Rader Detering, Publisher, Wooded Isle Press; Marie Poole, Financial Advisor and Consultant; and Liz Smith, Crowd Funding Campaign Manager. Your collaborative efforts and mutual support for one another and for me provided the necessary strength for me to stay focused and committed. The four of you never for one moment let go of your optimism and faith in me and the project. Your suggestions, guidance, various talents of the highest caliber, and insights proved to be invaluable in bringing my memoir to publication.

To my graphic designer, Naama Ozair, who in just one short meeting "got me" and what my memoir is truly about. Your graphic design eloquently and passionately expresses the meaning of being on a life journey towards redemption and living in truth.

To my proofreader, Marianne Tatom, for generously investing your time and energy in assuring that my "t's were crossed and i's were dotted," enhancing the quality of my message and affording easier readability.

To my incredible editor, Alys Yablon Wylen, for your uncanny and rare ability to enter both my heart and mind and help me tell my story so it has as much impact as imaginable. I am confident that I would not be at this juncture without you. With your talent, intelligence, and clear articulate ways, you have been essential in helping me develop this book from an idea to a completed work.

To the several holy brothers and sisters who have welcomed me back to Israel, to Jerusalem, and most importantly to your lives. You know who you are, and I remain eternally grateful to you for your openness of heart and soul.

To all of you, thank you for believing in the importance of sharing my memoir with the world. Thank you for your love, respect, and enthusiasm, which always inspired me to move ahead and not look back. Your support, in all its many expressions, messages clearly the value in the telling of one's story and how it can help so many other people.

And most importantly and essentially, to my Creator, to HaShem, the Divine Presence in the world, and in each one of us: I remain forever grateful to You for the infinite love, compassion, and guidance with which You have abundantly blessed me and with which You continue to do on the path of my soul journey.

With God's help and abundant blessings, it surely takes a village to raise a child, and as well to birth a dream. I feel incredibly blessed and humbled to be immersed in such a beautiful village.

TO MY GENEROUS AND KIND BACKERS

THANK YOU FOR SUPPORTING THE WRITING AND PUBLICATION OF MY MEMOIR.

Steve & Nance Adler
Anonymous
Cecile & Stephen Arnold
Deb Arnold
Jane Becker & Jason Kintzer
Chauncey & Shira Bell
Judith Bender
Karen Binder
Erin Black
David & Jen Bolnick
Elizabeth Braverman & Phil Levin
Kevin Britt & Elisabeth Rosenthal
Gail B. Broder
Hadiyah Carlyle
Dr. Peter Chalit
Paige Chapel & Rhiannon Lombard
Wimsey Cherrington
Rosy Coe
Laurie Cogan
Margie Cogan
Andrew Cohen & James Packman
Barbara Levine Cohen
Shelly F Cohen
David & Robin Cohn
Congregation Tikvah Chadashah
Rebecca Corey & Joel Freedman
Elizabeth Davis
Ron DeChene & Robert Hovden
Julia Detering

Ruth Dick
Melissa Donahue & Katie Ladd
David Ewton & Veronica Minia
Sergey Feldman
Rebecca Finkel
Danyel Fisher & Kim Stedman
Dr. David & Tracey Flum
Shira Gazman
Peggy Gladner
Joel A Goldstein
Sam Greenberg
Linda Gromko, MD
David Gross & Kelly Sweet
Cherie Hershman & Mick Ostroff
Edith Horn
Diane Hostetler
Roz Houtman & Jay Parker
Jordana Rene Huchital
Beth Huppin
Pat Hurshell
Lance Jason
Brian Judd
Issy Kantor
Lynn Katz
Charna Klein
Keith Krivitzky
Stacy Lawson
Avi & Yocheved Leeker
Margaret Lemberg
Tamar Libicki
Natan and Chanan Van Herpen Meir
Marilyn Meyer
Daphne Minkoff & Noah Tratt

Amy Denburg Mook
Bill Mowat
Larry Nicholas & Thomas Underhill
Lisa Orlick-Salka & Corey Salka
Marie Poole
Liz Richmond
Pat Ronald
Joan Rothaus
Helene Russ & Larry Zuckerman
Amira Saba
Alison Sands
Brianna Sayres
Rachel Schachter
Amy Schottenstein
Kim Schulze
David & Wendy Schwartz
Paul Schwartz
Amee & Michael Sherer
Meira Shupack
Arthur Slepian
Lori Smith
Brad & Ellen Spear
Linda Sprague
Melissa Grace Stern
Doris Stiefel
Mark & Sheryl Stiefel
Betty Sussman
Dina Tanners
Marianne Tatom
Dana Tell & Ellie Weiss
Sarah Walsh
Ami & Aliza Weisz

Sharon Whiteman
Andrew Wilks
Danielle Yancey
Jessica Zehavi